FLOWER LORE AND LEGEND

BOTANICAL FOLKLORE

First Edition 1917
Katharine M. Beals

New Edition 2019
Edited by Tarl Warwick

FLOWER LORE AND LEGEND

COPYRIGHT AND DISCLAIMER

The first edition of this work is in the public domain having been written prior to 1925. This edition, with its cover art and format, is all rights reserved.

In no way may this text be construed as encouraging or condoning any harmful or illegal act. In no way may this text be construed as able to diagnose, treat, cure, or prevent any disease, injury, symptom, or condition.

FLOWER LORE AND LEGEND

FOREWORD

This following work is an excellent occult primer when it comes to botanical lore- it is also, variously, a collection of floral poetry and history, as well as contemporary lore regarding flowers and plants in general. This is a subject of extreme interest- the herbal has returned in the lexicon of modern medicine, floral décor has returned in some degree of vogue in interior decoration, and the flower as a potent symbol of fertility is certainly nowhere sparing, especially in some cultures.

Much of the material here is poetic- each section opens with a verse or two from some poet or another on the topic of flowers. These range from symbols of love (or lust!) to toxic species that represent various dangers. Regardless of the specific usage and form, they are all spoken of, often by Shakespeare, among others, and into then-modernity, in the early 20th century. It is a deep work, generally, and provides a fairly large number of species, and for each species, a fairly large number of inclusions about the spiritual and literary usage of the flower at hand. Perhaps the mandrake, clover, and rose here are of greatest overall interest to those of us intrigued by magic in its more literal sense, but every species here is of symbolic and poetic import.

This edition of "Flower Lore and Legend" has been carefully edited for format and word usage. Care has been taken to retain all original intent and meaning.

FLOWER LORE AND LEGEND

By Mary Howitt

"God might have bade the earth bring forth
Enough for great and small,
The oak tree and the cedar tree,
Without a flower at all.
We might have had enough, enough,
For every want of ours,
For luxury, medicine, and toil,
And yet have had no flowers.

Then wherefore, wherefore were they made,
All dyed with rainbow light,
All fashioned with supremest grace,
Up-springing day and night-
Springing in valleys green and low,
And on the mountains high,
And in the silent wilderness
Where no man passes by?

Our outward life requires them not-
Then wherefore had they birth?
To minister delight to man,
To beautify the earth;
To comfort man, to whisper hope,
Whene'er his faith is dim,
For who so careth for the flowers,
Will care much more for Him!"

FLOWER LORE AND LEGEND

THE SNOWDROP

FRIENDSHIP IN ADVERSITY- CONSOLATION- HOPE

> "Lone flower, hemmed in with snows, and white as they,
> But hardier far, once more I see thee bend
> Thy forehead, as if fearful to offend,
> Like an unbidden guest; though day by day,
> Storms, sallying from the mountain tops waylay
> The rising sun, and on the plains descend;
> Yet thou art welcome, welcome as a friend
> Whose zeal outruns his promise!"

Wordsworth, To a Snowdrop.

As our first parents turned away from the closed gates of the Garden of Eden the whole world looked bleak and cold. The trees were bare, the grass was brown, and the driving snow seemed to wrap the earth, as in a pall. All Nature seemed to mourn for the fall of man. Eve, overcome with the remembrance of all that she had lost, sank weeping to the ground. Her sorrow touched the heart of the Father, and He sent an angel to console her. As the angel was speaking, bidding her take heart and be of good courage, a snow flake fell upon her hand. Raising it to his face he breathed upon it and bade it take form and bud and blossom. Before it reached the earth it had been transformed into a beautiful plant with dainty drooping white blossoms. Smiling, the angel said to Eve, "Be of good cheer. Let this flower be to you an earnest of the sunshine and summer that will come again." Then, his mission being accomplished, the angel ascended to Heaven; but where he had been standing, sprang up, through the show, quantities of the white blossoms. This is the legend of how the snowdrop came to earth:

FLOWER LORE AND LEGEND

> "And the snowdrop, like the bow
> That spans the cloudy sky,
> Became a symbol whence we know,
> That brighter days are nigh."

The snowdrops are among the daintiest and the earliest of the spring flowers. They often bloom before the snow is gone. Florists have done their best to produce them for Christmas, but have never profitably succeeded. They are cosmopolitan and will grow almost everywhere, except in extreme tropical countries, but are at their best on the Caucasian Mountains and in Asia Minor. Although they grow wild in England and Europe, in America they are generally found among the cultivated flowers. The Latin name, given to the plant by Linnaeus, is calanthus, meaning milk-flower. The family name is amaryllis. Its nicknames are numerous.

In Germany it is called February flower, snow violet, and naked maiden; in France, white-bell, bell-of-the-snow, winter-bell, and snow-piercer. The English name, snowdrop, is said to have been derived from the German, and the drop refers to the long pendants which were worn, in their ears, by the women of the fifteenth and sixteenth centuries. They are often seen in portraits by the Dutch and Italian painters of that period, and have been revived as ornaments at various times since. The popular Danish name for the flower is sommer gorrk, meaning summer fool. Hans Christian Andersen tells a pathetic story of the sommer gorrk, who, deceived by the bright sunshine and in a hurry to don her dainty spring gown, started from her warm home in the earth, and against the advice of her friends, forced her way through the snow, confident that she would eventually reach the summer land.

Struggling for a time against the cold and snow, her delicate robes stained and draggled, she found no other flowers

FLOWER LORE AND LEGEND

to keep her company and finally was beaten down by a storm of sleet and wind, while only a little distance to the southward, flooding the fields with sunshine, summer was drawing nearer and nearer every day to the poor little perishing blossom. The dear old story-teller likens to the sommer gorrk those noble souls, born into a world not yet prepared to receive them- the reformers, who are reviled and persecuted by their own generations, but who are later held in honor,- the poets, the scientists, and the statesmen, who are only recognized by posterity. These, he says, are sommer gorrks. How many dreamers, like the snowdrops, are the prophets of the spring!

Among the Russian folk-tales, there is one which tells how the snowdrop came to be the first flower of spring. A beautiful girl was left, at the death of her father, to the care of a cruel stepmother, whose own daughter was extremely jealous. Between them the poor girl was badly treated. At last, urged by her daughter, the stepmother determined to get rid of the girl. It was January. The snow was deep and a freezing cold wind blew from the mountains. Calling the girl, she sent her out into the forest, bidding her not to return until she could bring back a bunch of snowdrops. Sorrowfully, the maiden went out into the storm, on her hopeless errand. As she entered the wood she saw far ahead, among the leafless trees, a fire burning brightly, about which were twelve stones, and seated on the stones twelve men. The chief, sitting on the largest stone, was an old man, with a long white beard, who held a staff in his hand. The girl timidly approached and observing that she was almost frozen, after the men had made room for her at the fire, the chief inquired why she was out in the forest in such inclement weather. With many tears, she told him her sad story and after a glance around the circle he said slowly: "I am January. I cannot give you any snowdrops, but perhaps my brother February can help you," and turning to a fine young man sitting near him he continued: "Brother February, you may sit in my place." In a little while,

FLOWER LORE AND LEGEND

after they had exchanged seats, the ice and snow around the fire began to melt, a softness came into the air and at the feet of February, up through the snow came the flower buds. Presently a bed of snowdrops was in full bloom. The young girl thanked her hosts, gathered a beautiful bouquet, and carried it home to her astonished and frightened stepmother.

During the Crimean War, when the allied forces were encamped before Sebastopol, and the long severe winter brought terrible privation and suffering to the troops, the soldiers watched and longed for some sign of the breaking of the winter. One day, in the latter part of February, a trooper came excitedly running into a tent, where a number of his comrades sat sadly thinking of home and friends. In his hand he held two or three small white flowers. "Look, look," he cried, "spring snowdrops!" The men arose to their feet, uncovered their heads to the white blossoms, the first sign of returning spring, and wept like little children. From that time their courage revived rapidly, as day by day they searched for the bright little flowers. When they returned to England many of them brought with them bulbs of the plant, which had been to them such a joy. Thus the variety, known as the Crimean snowdrop, was introduced into England. The bees are very fond of this flower. The blossoms only remain open about six hours every day, from ten in the morning until four in the afternoon, but during that short time they are a Godsend to the few honey-bees who, almost in winter, have been tempted to stray into the sunshine. The honey is protected from the snow and rain by the drooping position of the flowers and the perfume of the blossom is a guide which directs the venturesome insects to the good cheer that awaits them. It would be remarkable if a flower so appropriate for religious symbolism had not been made use of in that connection. The fact that the snowdrop was often found, in abundance, in the old convent gardens, led to the belief that it was sacred to virgins.

FLOWER LORE AND LEGEND

Thus it was dedicated to the Virgin Mary. On the second of February, Candlemas day, when the Feast of the Purification of the Blessed Virgin is celebrated in commemoration of the presentation of the Child Jesus, by His parents, in the Jewish Temple, the statue of the Virgin having been removed from the altar, the place where it stood is strewn with snowdrops, the emblems of purity and chastity. In some places it became customary for young women, wearing white gowns, to walk in procession, carrying snowdrops in their hands. An old saying serves to remind us of this:

> "The snowdrop in purest white array,
> First rears her head on Candlemas day."

Although the snowdrop has most appropriately been regarded as an emblem of purity, of hope, of consolation, and of courage in Germany and some parts of England, it was considered a forecast of death to bring the first snowdrop into the house. Other superstitions in regard to the flower were more pleasing. It was often said that any one wearing a snowdrop would have only pure and lofty thoughts; and that if a young girl ate the first snowdrop she found in the spring neither sun nor wind would tan her that summer. The flower seems to have been a favorite with many writers, and, although there is no recorded bibliography, there is little difficulty in finding abundant tributes. No plant brings to mind more associations. All flowers command admiration, but it compels affection. The women poets of England have all loved it. In their verses, Mrs. Barbauld, Mrs. Browning, and Mrs. Hemans have told us of their regard. Montgomery calls it the "Morning Star of Flowers." Rossetti writes of the pendulous blossoms with the "heart-shaped seal of green." Barry Cornwall, referring to its associations, says it is the emblem of friendship in adversity, and is protected by an armor all its own.

FLOWER LORE AND LEGEND

"Thou first born of the year's delight
Pride of the dewy glade,
In vernal green and virgin white
Thy vestal robes arrayed
They twinkle to the wintry moon
And cheer the ungenial day,
And tell us all will glisten soon
As green and bright as they."

Keble, To the Snowdrop,

FLOWER LORE AND LEGEND

THE ARBUTUS

YOU ONLY DO I LOVE

"There is a flower whose name I need not call,
Which shyly hides beside the crumbling wall,
Or lifts, through drifts of leaves, her modest head
And looks about, and asks, "Is winter dead?"

Anonymous.

In England, the hawthorn is universally known as mayflower, or may; but in America, especially in New England, that name is given to the fragrant pink-and-white blossoms of the arbutus. After that first terrible winter which the Pilgrim Fathers spent on the stern coast at Plymouth, as the spring approached, and the snow melted, bare spots appeared on the summit and sides of Burial Hill. From under the dead grass and melting ice, clinging closely to the ground, peeped the bright leaves and clusters of its delicate blossoms, harbingers of spring. No wonder that those early pioneers, grave and austere as they were, loved them and called them mayflowers. The good ship, which had brought them hither, was also thus honored. The Greek name given by Linnaeus is epigaea repens, which means creeping on the earth. It belongs exclusively to the new world and has no classic associations, yet is not altogether without tradition.

Among the legends of the Iroquois is found the story of its birth. Long, long ago, before the white man had set foot on the shore of the new world, an old man lived alone in a tepee, in one of the forests near the great lakes. His beard and hair were long and white. He was dressed in skins of the beaver. A bearskin hung before the door of his lodge, for it was winter, and snow and ice were everywhere. The nearby stream was frozen over and the wind moaned through the tree-tops of the forest. One night after he had been abroad in the wood, picking up broken branches and roots of trees that he might keep up his fire, as the wind blew and the snow drifted against his door, he cried out loudly, protesting that all must perish. Suddenly, the bearskin that hung before his door was pushed aside and a beautiful maiden entered. Her cheeks were like roses, her eyes were bright, and her hair was as black as the crow's wing. She wore a mantle of sweet grass and ferns and on her head was a wreath of flowers. As she entered, the whole lodge seemed filled with warmth and perfume. The old man gazed in wonder at the fair visitor, and said; "Welcome, my daughter, to this poor shelter; my fire is low, but draw near and tell me whence come you and who are thy people, and I will tell thee of my victories."

The maiden smiled and the dark little lodge seemed filled with brightness. The old man took down his pipe and when he had filled and lighted it, he began: "I am Manito, the Great. The breath of my nostrils causes the waters in the rivers and the lakes to stand still in frozen silence."

The maiden replied: "Manito is great, but when I smile, flowers spring up everywhere and the fields are carpeted with green."

Then said Manito: "When I shake my hoary locks, the earth is wrapped in a snowy pall, the leaves fall from the trees, the birds fly before my breath, and the winds wail all over the land."

"Oh, Manito is very great," said the maiden, "more terrible is he than the red man; but, as I pass along, the leaves cover the branches which thou hast laid bare, the birds sing, and the breeze is soft and pleasant."

FLOWER LORE AND LEGEND

As the maiden was speaking, Manito heard not. His head had dropped on his breast; his pipe had fallen from his hand, and he was sleeping. The maiden waved her hands. His head began to shrink and streams of water ran down from his long locks and beard; his garments turned into green leaves, and birds flew into the lodge singing their sweet songs. The maiden took from her bosom some beautiful fragrant flowers, white and rose-pink, and hid them under the leaves that had sprung up about her feet, and before she put them there she kissed them and said, "I give to thee, all my beauty, my sweetness, and my most fragrant breath, and men shall gather thee with bowed heads and on bended knee." Then she passed on over the fields and up the hills. Everywhere the birds, the winds, and the brooks greeted her with a joyous song, and wherever she stepped, but nowhere else, grows the arbutus to this day.

Mrs. Whitman wrote these lines:

"There's a flower that grows by the greenwood tree,
In its desolate beauty more dear to me
Than all that bask in the noontide beam
Through the long, bright summer by font and stream,
Like a pure hope nursed beneath sorrow's wing
Its timid buds from the cold moss spring,
Their delicate hues like the pink sea shell
Or the shaded blush of the hyacinth's bell,
Their breath more sweet than the faint perfume
That breathes from the bridal orange-bloom."

Whenever the choice of a national flower has been under discussion, it has been a prominent candidate, and in 1909 it was the leader in a contest among the school children of Wisconsin, as their choice, for a state flower. In some parts of that state it has become customary to call a certain day in the spring Arbutus day. Under the supervision of a committee of club women, the children gather, and in conveyances contributed, and in many cases driven by the farmers, go out into the woods in search of the blossoms. On their return, the flowers are packed in boxes and sent to Milwaukee and other large cities to be distributed as the committee decides.

There has been much criticism of this wholesale gathering and fears have been expressed that before many years the plant may have become only a memory. It is already practically exterminated in New York state, where once it grew in abundance. It does not bear transplanting well, nor does it thrive in any but a wild state. It is becoming more restricted in territory and scarcer every year. Suggestions have been made that laws be enacted for the protection of our vanishing wild flowers like those for the protection of game and fish. The trailing arbutus grows only in North America. It is the national flower of Newfoundland and is found along the eastern coast as far south as Florida and as far west as Minnesota, where, however, it is rare, growing only in territory adjacent to Duluth, on the Kettle River, and in the valley of the St. Croix.

The arbutus or strawberry tree, which is mentioned by Pliny, belongs to the same family and has many of the characteristics of its less imposing relative. It has the same smooth red bark and glossy evergreen foliage. The blossoms are the same, only larger. It was used by the Romans with other symbolic trees and flowers at the festival of Pales, the goddess of pastoral life, and was dedicated to Candia, the sister of Apollo, who used a rod from this tree to drive away witches and to protect children from illness and witchcraft. The fruit was of the size and appearance of the strawberry, but ripened so slowly, that, like the orange tree, fruit and blossom occupied the tree at the same time. Pliny gave it the name unedo, because it was so bitter that "he who ate once, would eat no more."

FLOWER LORE AND LEGEND

In Spain and Italy, however, it is still an article of food. It is said to resemble cranberries in flavor, for which it is sometimes used as a substitute. The Abbe Barthelemy, in his Travels of Anacharsis, describes these trees as they grew on the summit of Mt. Ida, in Crete. This oriental arbutus was frequently referred to by ancient writers. Horace celebrated it in his odes, and, in the Aeneid, the bier of Pallas is described by Virgil as covered with arbutus rods and oaken twigs. Numerous other allusions are made to it by the classic poets. Tributes to the mayflower or trailing arbutus have been generally confined to American writers and almost every New England author has at some time written affectionately of the sweet-scented blossoms. Thoreau, John Burroughs, and Higginson, among prose writers, have given it especial mention, and a volume of some size might be compiled from the poems written of the modest little flower. Perhaps the best-known verses are by Whittier, who writes of the mayflower and the pilgrims:

> "God be praised!" the pilgrim said,
> Who saw the blossoms peer
> Above the brown leaves, dry and dead,
> Behold our mayflower here.
>
> O sacred flowers of faith and hope,
> As sweetly now, as then,
> Ye bloom on many a birchen slope,
> In many a pine-dark glen.
>
> So live the fathers in their sons,
> Their sturdy faith be ours,
> And ours the love that overruns
> Its rocky strength with flowers."

Whittier, The Mayflowers,

FLOWER LORE AND LEGEND

THE CROCUS

CHEERFULNESS

"Hail to the King of Bethlehem!
Who weareth in His diadem
A yellow crocus for the gem
Of His authority."

Longfellow, Golden Legend.

In England and North America, the little purple pasque-flower, which the children call gosling, that pushes its way almost through the snowdrifts and is so abundant on our hillsides in the springtime, is often incorrectly called crocus. Some botanists class it in the anemone family. Professor Conway McMillan calls it a species of clematis. The crocus of ancient times was of a bright yellow color and corresponded to our marsh marigold. It was also known by the name of saffron, which is still used to describe a peculiarly brilliant shade of yellow. Readers of Homer will remember that he uses the epithet saffron-robed to describe the glory of the dawn. In Egypt, the expression saffron-colored served to convey an idea of the brilliancy of the setting sun.

The ancients regarded the crocus as dedicated to Helios, the Sun-God. In the Middle Ages the flower was thought to belong especially to St. Valentine. Some writers say that the name is from a Greek word meaning thread, because the fiber of the plant was used in dyeing brilliant yellow, which was a favorite color of the Greeks, as well as other Eastern nations. The Greeks had a tradition as to the origin of the plant. According to their mythology, Crocus was a noble youth who was very much in love with a beautiful shepherdess named Smilax. According

FLOWER LORE AND LEGEND

to the laws of the gods, he could not marry her and in his disappointment he killed himself. Smilax was heart-broken and wept so much that Flora, the goddess, felt sorry for her and turned them both into plants; Crocus into the flower that bears his name, and Smilax into a beautiful vine, the tendrils of which were used to bind together garlands of the crocus used by the Greeks as decorations at their marriage festivals.

There is also an autumnal variety. This has been sweetly referred to in verse:

> "Say what impels amid surrounding snow
> Congealed the crocus' flamy bud to grow?
> Say what retards amid the summer's blaze
> The autumnal bud 'til pale declining days?"

The plant has many medicinal qualities. Pliny enumerates over twenty remedies derived from it. According to his natural history, those using it as a drink will never suffer from indigestion or headache. He also says that it was regarded as hindering intoxication and as a fine tonic for the heart and lungs. In the time of pestilence and plague, it was used as a preventive. Its wreaths, worn on the head, were said to dispel the fumes of wine. The Egyptians wreathed their wine cups with its garlands for the same purpose. It was used extensively by the Jews as an aromatic, and is referred to by Solomon in Canticles 4-14, as one of the plants in the delectable garden. The Greeks used it also for perfume, while the Romans were so fond of its odor that they decorated their homes and public assembly houses with it, and at banquets small streams of its essence were made to issue from fountains and to descend on the guests in a fine spray. As it was thought to inspire love, potions were made from it. It was said to bloom at dawn on St. Valentine's day.

The coloring matter made from the fiber of the plant has

FLOWER LORE AND LEGEND

long been used in cooking. Shakespeare, in A Winter's Tale, speaks of its use to color the warden-pies. At present it serves to color confectionery. The controversy as to the introduction of the plant into England has at times waxed fiercely, but it is now generally conceded that Sir Thomas Smith first imported it from Persia about the middle of the fourteenth century. There is a tradition current at Saffron-Walden, in Cambridgeshire, where the plant was first cultivated, that it was brought by a pilgrim, who wished to render some service to his country. He had his staff made hollow, and in this way brought a root into England at the risk of his life. If he had been discovered, according to the law of Persia, he would have been put to death. Many beautiful poems have been written about the crocus. The French poet, Rapin, has beautifully told its story and Virgil tells of the fondness of the bees for the "glowing crocus." Moore, in Lalla Rookh, sings of the same thing. Almost all of the New England poets have a word in praise for the "brave little crocus," while present-day writers do not neglect it, as the following, taken from the Westminster Gazette, will prove:

> "O, you plucky fellows, All in sunshine yellows,
> Braving bitter winds and cold, Waving fearless flags of gold,
> Welcome, crocus fellows! Hardships and privation,
> Sleet and snow for ration, Leave you laughing, gay and bold,
> Grieve you little- faith untold, Mocks at mere privation.
> Welcome, comrade fellows, All in sunshine yellows!
> Still your cups of light unfold, Out of clay your glory mold!
> Welcome, plucky fellows! Anon, Yellow Crocuses."

FLOWER LORE AND LEGEND

THE ANEMONE

WITHERED HOPES

"Youth, like a thin anemone, displays
His silken leaf, and in a morn decays."

Sir William Jones.

Although it is one of the earliest of the spring blossoms, the anemone is not a cheerful flower. It withers almost as soon as it is gathered. In Sweden there is a saying that it blooms in the wood when the swallow returns from his winter migration. The name, anemone, or wind-flower, some writers claim, was given it because it is so fragile that it withers when the wind blows over it; others say that it only blooms when the wind blows it open. The classical legend as to the origin of the plant is based upon both suppositions.

One day Cupid was playing with his mother, Venus, and he accidentally wounded her in the breast with one of his arrows. Before the wound had healed, Adonis crossed her path and she forgot everything for him. Adonis loved to hunt and Venus, who was rather indolent and not inclined to exert herself, put on hunting garments and roamed through the woods like Diana. She was much alarmed lest Adonis should be injured in an encounter with some wild beast, and gave him continual warnings not to put himself in danger and especially not to attack bears or lions as they were his mortal enemies. Adonis was a brave youth, and laughed at her fears, and when a wild boar one day sprang from its lair and attacked the dogs that were with him, he threw his spear and wounded the animal. The beast turned and buried its tusks in his side, causing instant death. Venus, at this moment passing through the air in her chariot drawn by white swans, saw

FLOWER LORE AND LEGEND

the body bathed in blood lying on the ground. Stopping her chariot, she alighted and reproaching the Fates, exclaimed: "You have taken away my love, but you shall have but a partial triumph!" Weeping over the dead body, she said: "Your blood shall be transformed into a flower that shall blossom every spring as a memorial of my grief." Then she sprinkled nectar over the blood, and in an hour there sprang up a delicate flower with crimson-veined petals. Because the wind blows them open, and soon after blows them away, it is called the anemone, or wind-flower. It is said to have been dedicated to Venus because of her tears.

Another story is that Anemone was the name of a beautiful nymph whom Zephyr loved very dearly. Flora becoming very jealous exiled her from court, but when she pined away and died of a broken heart Zephyr importuned Venus, who changed her body into the flower which bears the name, and Zephyr is said to fan her all the day long with his wings. The flower poet, Rapin, concludes his account of the transformation, with these words:

> "So the fair victim fell, whose beauty's light
> Had been more lasting, had it been less bright;
> She, though transformed, as charming as before,
> The fairest maid is now the fairest flower."

Although the anemone is a classical flower and dedicated to Venus, it also has a place among the fairy plants. The painting of its delicate veins is ascribed to those little creatures. The botanists describe the flower as a natural barometer, because as the night approaches, or just before a shower, the dampness in the air causes the petals to curl over tent fashion, but fairy-lore tells us that this is done by the fairies who cuddle down in the heart of the flower and pull the leaves over them like curtains. Pliny, who wrote a natural history sometime during the first century, which treats of almost everything under the sun, attributes medicinal properties to the plant. He says that it is good for pains and inflammation in the head; that, if the root is chewed, it will cure the toothache; that a decoction made from the leaves is very beneficial to the eyes. The Eastern magicians regarded the plant as a preventive of sickness, and recommended every one to gather the first blossom that is seen in the spring, repeating very solemnly the words, "I gather thee as a remedy against disease." Afterwards it must be wrapped in a red cloth and carefully kept in a dark place. If the person who gathered the flower was taken ill, it was to be tied around the neck or under the arm. The Egyptians regarded it as an emblem of sickness. In some countries it is thought that the blossoms taint the air and cause severe illness. In some parts of North America, at the present time, they are regarded as unwholesome for cattle to eat.

They are said to have sprung up in England from the blood of Danes, who were slain in battle. The Romans planted them at High Cross, near Leicester, as a charm against dropsy. But wherever they are found they do not bloom until the wind calls. A New England poetess, Lucy Larcom, thus expresses it:

> "'Why have I come here?' the windflower said.
> 'Why?' and she gracefully nodded her head.
> The storm rocked my cradle with lullaby wild,
> 'I am here with the wind, because I am his child.'"

A story is told of a florist in Paris, who imported a very beautiful variety from the East Indies. He was so afraid that some one else would get the benefit of this prize that he guarded it most carefully, and for ten years succeeded in keeping it to himself. One day a French councilor visited the gardens when the plants were in seed, and, as he passed the bed in which they were growing, dropped his cloak on them. A number of the seeds clung to the woolen surface of the garment, and his servant, to

FLOWER LORE AND LEGEND

whom he had previously given instructions, picked up the cloak 'and folded it up without attracting attention. The councilor sharing the seed with his friends broke up the monopoly. An armorial device was sent to one of the noted beauties of the seventeenth century with the suggestion that she adopt it as her own. The shield bore the frail anemone, with the motto, "Brevis est usus." (Her reign is short, or literally, 'Short is its use.')

The short life of the flower has served poets of all ages for a text upon the brevity of life. Shakespeare writes: "These flowers are like the pleasures of the world," and the following lines are by the English poet, Pratt:

> "Sweet are the memories that ye bring,
> Of the pleasant leafy woods of spring;
> Of the wild bee, so gladly humming,
> Joyous that earth's young flowers are coming;
> Of the nightingale and merry thrush,
> Cheerfully singing from every bush;
> And the cuckoo's note, when the air is still,
> Heard far away on the distant hill."

Pratt, Spring.

FLOWER LORE AND LEGEND

THE NARCISSUS

SELF-LOVE

"And narcissi, the finest among them all,
Who gaze on their eyes in the stream's recess
Till they die of their own dear loveliness."

Shelley.

Echo was a beautiful nymph who had one very great fault, she always would have the last word. One day Jupiter, the father of the Roman gods, who was called Zeus by the Greeks, was watching the naiads dancing in the woods when Juno came looking for him. Echo, knowing that the fun would be spoiled, met her and by her sprightly conversation detained the goddess until the nymphs could make their escape to another spot. When Juno discovered this, she was very angry and passed sentence upon Echo: "You shall forfeit the power of speech, except for the purpose of repeating the last word you hear..." Now in Bœotia there lived a beautiful youth of whom it had been foretold that he should live happily until he beheld his own face. His name was Narcissus. As he was pursuing the chase one day, Echo beheld him and fell in love with him; but, alas! she could not speak to him, and could only repeat the last word that he said. Narcissus grew angry and left her, and poor Echo pined away until there was nothing left but her voice. Then her sister nymphs begged Diana to cause this careless youth to know sometime what it meant to love and meet with no return. Diana, with whom Echo was a favorite, granted their prayer, and Cupid, who is always ready, assisted.

One day, as Narcissus, who had never loved any one, was wandering among the hills, he came to a beautiful pool of

FLOWER LORE AND LEGEND

water and, bending down to take a drink, he saw his own face reflected in the clear surface. He thought it was some water spirit, and immediately fell in love with his own reflection. But alas! the vision fled at his touch. He spoke, but it did not answer. "When I beckon you do the same, but you come no nearer," he cried, and he would not leave the shore of the pool, but wandered about in the woods near by, weeping. The beauty which had so charmed Echo faded away, and at length he died, knowing what it was to love without return. The water nymphs mourned for him and prepared a funeral pyre, but when they would have buried the body it had disappeared and in its place was a beautiful flower with a yellow center, which they named Narcissus, in his memory. In the cup in the center, it is said, the tears of the ill-fated youth may be found.

Old Ben Jonson retold the story in his verse:

"Arise, and speak thy sorrows, Echo; arise
Here by this fountain, where thy love did pine,
Whose memory lives fresh to lasting fame,
Shrined in this yellow flower that bears his name."

Near a clear spring, in an open space in the midst of the woods, where tendrils creep and the blue sky looks down from above, the blossom, forlorn in its drooping loveliness, may still be found. Keats sings that:

"Grieving by the pool
His spreading ringers shoot in verdant leaves;
Through his pale veins green sap now gently flows,
And in a short-lived flower his beauty blows.
Let vain Narcissus warn each female breast
That beauty's but a transient good at best."

Echo still roams the woods and when the children call

FLOWER LORE AND LEGEND

she hopes it is Narcissus, and they hear her answer as she searches for him. There is probably no place in the world where the white narcissi grow so abundantly, in a wild state, as on the slopes of the mountains that overlook the castle of Chillon, in Switzerland. It has been the custom from time immemorial for crowds of visitors to go to Montreux in the springtime for the pleasure of gathering these flowers. About 1896, the town authorities determined to utilize this custom. On the 19th and 20th of May is celebrated the 'Fete des Narcisse.' Thousands of spectators crowd the great amphitheater, in the English garden. On the wide platform is grouped a large chorus of Alpine singers, draped in dark cloaks and singing a weird air. They represent the earth in the winter time. Then follows a strain of cheery music and a party of winter visitors appear, clothed in costumes of various nations, and girls in Italian dresses offer their roses, but Montreux has something better. The brown hoods of the chorus are thrown back and garlands of green appear. Birds come flying in, by machinery; the brown cloaks drop, and the singers are seen all in green and white representing the narcissus. The Sun King comes in his chariot of gold, and birds and flowers all join in singing the welcome to spring.

The white or poet's narcissus is edged with pink and represents youthful purity and beauty attuned by fragrance. The innocence displayed in its large soft eye is rarely rivaled among the flowers. It is an emblem of the Virgin Mother. In England one variety is called the daffodil. It wears a yellow instead of a white dress, and as the children say:

> "Daff a down dill has come to town,
> In a yellow petticoat and a green gown."

In some parts, because it reaches its prime during the month of March, it is known as the Lentlily, and also by the more homely name of butter and eggs. In China it is called shin sin fa, which means water fairy flower. The Persians know it as golden and the Turks call it the golden bowl. The daffodil is supposed to be one of the flowers that Proserpina was gathering when she was seized and carried away by Pluto, who was a brother of Jupiter and King of the Infernal Regions. One day he saw Proserpina among the goddesses and fell in love with her. He determined to have her for his wife, but he knew that her mother, Ceres, the goddess of agriculture, would never allow her daughter to go with him to the under world. He consulted Venus, who promised to aid him.

One day Proserpina was gathering flowers by a beautiful lake in the Vale of Enna, where it is always spring. Her mother, who was resting on the shore of the lake, warned her not to wander far, but Venus caused beautiful flowers to keep springing up just ahead of the girl, enticing her further and further away. Pluto, who was watching her, suddenly appeared in his chariot with coal-black horses, caught her and carried her off. She screamed for help, but Ceres did not hear her, and the chariot and its occupants vanished through an opening in the earth. As it disappeared, Proserpina dropped some of the flowers she had been gathering. Daffodils are said to have been the flowers with which Venus tempted her to wander, and which she dropped from the chariot. We are told that the heavy perfume of the flowers dulled the senses of Ceres so that she did not perceive her daughter's danger; and Proserpina, herself, was so overcome by the narcotic influence of the blossoms that she did not realize what was happening to her.

Jean Ingelow wrote:

"Lo! one she marked of rarer growth
Than orchis or anemone;
For it the maiden left them both,
And parted from her company.

FLOWER LORE AND LEGEND

> Drawn nigh, she deemed it fairer still,
> And stooped to gather by the rill
> The daffodil, the daffodil."

In literature the daffodil has a prominent place. Jean Ingelow has beautifully told this story in her poem of Persephone. Shakespeare, in A Winter's Tale, thus refers to it:

> "Oh, Proserpina,
> For the flowers now that frightened thou let'st fall
> From Dis's wagon, Daffodils
> That come before the swallow dares- and take
> The winds of March with beauty."

Ancient writers did not neglect this beautiful flower, although they refer to it often, on account of its narcotic properties, as an emblem of deceitfulness. Homer asserts that it delights heaven and earth with its odor and beauty, and at the same time induces stupor, and sometimes death. Among the later writers the daffodil is a favorite, and many verses have been written in praise of it, among the best known being those by Herrick:

> "Faire Daffodils, we weep to see
> You haste away so soone;
> As yet the early-rising sun
> Has not attain'd his noone.
> Stay, stay,
> Until the hasting day
> Has run
> But to the even song;
> And, having pray'd together, we
> Will goe with you along.
>
> We have short time to stay as you.

FLOWER LORE AND LEGEND

> We have as short a spring;
> As quick a growth to meet decay,
> As you, or any thing.
> We die,
> As your hours doe, and drie
> Away
> Like to the summer's rains,
> Or as the pearles of morning's dew
> Ne'er to be found againe."

Some say that the daffodil was the ancient asphodel and that its name is a corruption of that word. Dr. Prior thinks it sounds like saffron lily, while Lady Wilkinson derives it from the old word affodyle, which means "it cometh early." Generally, it is thought to be "the rose of Sharon."

The Romans built altars and offered sacrifices at springs of pure water. Thus the fountain nymphs were honored by the Fontinalian ceremonies. In England daffodils were thrown into the rivers on Holy Thursday, and it is thought that the custom was a survival from these old rites. Milton in Comus refers to the practice.

> "Carol her good deeds loud in rustic lays
> And throw sweet garland wreaths into her stream,
> Of pansies, pinks and daffodils."

The jonquil is another variety of the same family. The science of language tells us that the name was conferred upon the narcissus from the Greek word narka, which means numbness, and is the root of the word narcotic. By its use medicinally torpor can be produced. There are about twenty varieties of the plant. They are marked by a cup, like a drinking glass, which widens at the top, and are grown from bulbs.

FLOWER LORE AND LEGEND

Mahomet once said:

"He that has two cakes of bread, let him sell one for some flowers of the narcissus, for bread is the food of the body, but narcissus is the food of the soul."

Perhaps the most noted verses about this flower are those of Wordsworth. The line of another English poet: "A thing of beauty is a joy forever," has become a household proverb. It is found in connection with his reference to the daffodil:

"A thing of beauty is a joy forever.
Its loveliness increases. It will never
Pass into nothingness...
...Such the sun, the moon.
Trees old and young ; sprouting a shady boon
For simple sheep; and such are daffodils
With the green world they live in."

Keats, Endymion.

FLOWER LORE AND LEGEND

THE DANDELION

COQUETRY

"Dear common flower, that grow'st beside the way,
Fringing the dusty road with harmless gold,
First pledge of blithesome May,
Which children pluck and, full of pride, uphold."

"Gold, such as thine, ne'er drew the Spanish prow
Through the primeval hush of Indian seas,
Nor wrinkled the lean brow
Of age, to robe the lover's heart of ease:
Tis the spring's largess, which she scatters now
To rich and poor alike, with lavish hand,
Though most hearts never understand,
To take it at God's value, but pass by,
The offered wealth with unrewarded eye."

Lowell, To a Dandelion.

Once upon a time the world was inhabited by fairies. Brownies and elves were skipping about in the grass. The trees were the homes of the wood-gnomes. The cheerful little flower-sprites, in their gay colored gowns, were flitting about in the sunshine. Suddenly human giants appeared, and the heavy foot of man wrought havoc and destruction in fairy-land. The frightened little gnomes hid themselves deep in the earth. The elves sought shelter in crevices of the rocks. The brownies ran for the hollow trunks of trees. But the fairies loved the sunshine, and could not live in the dark ground nor hollow trees. The poor little things did not know where to hide themselves, and in their terror they clung to the stems of plants- each to the plant that was nearest- while the Queen changed them all into flowers of the color of the gowns they were wearing, and wherever there had been a fairy, there was then a flower.

That very morning a number of the fairies had appeared in new frocks, made of bright yellow sunbeams, and after all the excitement was over, these little people found themselves huddled close together on one stem, staring straight up at the sun. Botanists who do not know very much about fairies call this flower a composite; but every child knows that it is a real fairy family, and they are so kind and helpful to each other that all the little ones are put in the center, and the older and stronger ones form a circle around them for protection. By some very old authorities, this is said to have been the origin of the dandelion.

The 'gamin of the fields,' as the plant is sometimes called, is a native of Greece, and emigrated to this country, where it has made itself quite at home. It thrives under almost any conditions, although it prefers lanes and grassy fields. It blossoms during every month in the year, and is an interesting illustration of co-operation, the flower being composed of from one to two hundred tiny blossoms, each perfect in itself, and together demonstrating most forcibly that "in union there is strength."

It has managed without the aid of legislation to take possession of the soil in every part of the civilized world, and has so firmly established itself that any one who has tried to eradicate it from even one small lawn, although inclined to question the survival of the fittest, will be convinced that "never say die " is an appropriate motto. The name is derived from the French- dent de lion (a lion's tooth). In nearly every European country the plant bears a name of similar significance, presumably from its jagged leaf, which was thought to resemble the teeth of a lion, or from the root, which is very white, and thus like them. Some writers have associated the flower with the sun, and, as the lion was the animal symbol of that planet, have assumed that the flower received its name on that account.

Among the country people, in Switzerland, the flower is known as the shepherd's clock, because it opens at five o'clock in the morning and closes at eight in the evening. The shepherds, in the mountains, often use it to guess at the time of day. The feathery seed-balls which succeed the yellow blossom serve as a barometer to predict fine or stormy weather.

These seed-balls are also consulted by young men and maidens as oracles. A lover being separated from his sweetheart, would carefully pick one of the feathery blooms and, whispering a tender message for each one of the downy petals, would blow them toward the spot where the loved one was. The feathers always carry the messages faithfully. If a maiden wished to know if her lover was thinking of her, she took a dandelion that had gone to seed and blew away the down. If after three puffs there was a single feather left, she might rest assured that she was not forgotten. This oracle was also consulted as to whether there was a lover, whether he lived north or south, east or west, and whether he was coming or not. Sir Walter Scott refers to this superstition. To dream of dandelions foreboded misfortune and treachery on the part of some loved one. There are few children who have not at some time made long slender curls out of dandelion stems, and used the blow-balls to find out whether or not mother wanted them. The plant is often called a weed. If Emerson's definition of a weed is correct, "a plant whose virtues have not yet been discovered," this classification is incorrect, for the plant has many useful properties.

Under the name taraxacum, it has been an important factor in medicine from ancient times. Once it was held in high estimation as a remedy for consumption. Some medical authorities recommend it for dropsy, gastric derangement, and

FLOWER LORE AND LEGEND

various skin diseases.

It shelters itself from the sun's heat by closing its petals. Linnaeus enumerates forty-six flowers, and among them the dandelion, which protect themselves in a similar way, classifying them as meteoric, because they are affected by the atmosphere; as tropical, because they open and close earlier or later, as the length of the day increases or decreases; and as an equinoctial, because they open and close at a regular time. Mrs. Smith refers very prettily to this in her Floras Horologae?:

> "Thus in each flower and simple bell,
> That in our path betrodden lie,
> Are sweet remembrancers who tell
> How fast their winged moments fly."

It is said that if the dandelion down flies when there is no wind it is a sign of rain. The stems are playthings for the children. They cut them into short pieces and string them like beads, wearing them as necklaces or bracelets. Sometimes they are split and made into wonderful curls, which are attached to the heads of little girls. The common schools throughout the country used to close at four o'clock in the afternoon, and truant boys blowing thistledown from the stem found it safe to go home when four or more of the gossamer spines were left after one effective outpouring of the lungs. This practice has been referred to in verse:

> "Dandelion with globe of down
> The schoolboy's clock in every town,
> Which the truant puffs amain
> To conjure lost hours again."

The leaves are highly esteemed as a vegetable and for salad. The Apache Indians value them so highly that they will search the country for them for days, and the quantity that one individual will consume is almost beyond belief. In Germany, the roots are roasted and substituted for coffee by the peasants, and it is said that coffee made in this way can hardly be distinguished from that made from the real berry. Although it is such a common flower, it is a favorite with writers of both prose and poetry. Henry Ward Beecher in Star Papers speaks of them as "Golden kisses all over the cheeks of the meadow." Thoreau calls them the gold which he has on deposit in country banks, the interest on which is to be health and enjoyment. Lowell, in his Ode to a Dandelion, has given it a place in literature more exalted than that of many more aristocratic golden flowers. The difference between the glory of a dandelion in full bloom and the grave hoariness of its decay is very striking, and James Hurtis, an English poet, who died in 1801, made a fantastic use of this difference in his Village Curate. It was an original mind that could see in these two stages of a common weed the contrast between the flashy undergraduate and the grave divine of later years:

> "Dandelion this,
> A college youth that flashes for a day,
> All gold, anon, he doffs his gaudy suit,
> Touched by the magic hand of some grave bishop,
> And all at once becomes a reverent divine- how sleek."

> "But let me tell you in the pompous globe
> Which rounds the dandelion's head is couched
> Divinity most rare."

Hurtis, Village Curate.

FLOWER LORE AND LEGEND

THE LILY OF THE VALLEY

RETURN OF HAPPINESS

"No flower amid the garden fairer grows
Than the sweet lily of the lowly vale,
The queen of flowers."

Keats.

The Lily of the valley, or conval lily, is associated with religion and chivalry rather than mythology. In flower language it represents the return of happiness. With its beautiful blossoms, the rich green of its leaves, and its delicate fragrance, it is a fit harbinger of spring. In the Middle Ages, it was believed that it was the flower referred to by Christ when He bade the disciples consider the lilies of the field; but it is now conceded that the martagon, a tiger lily, was the lily of Palestine. The conval lily is an inhabitant of colder countries and is unknown in the dry, hot climate of the Holy Land. There is at least one legend as to the origin of the flower. About the year 559 a.d. there dwelt in the forest of Louvain, near Limoges, in France, a holy man known as St. Leonard. Having renounced all worldly things, he lived the life of a hermit in the depths of a wood. A huge dragon, representing temptation, also dwelt there, and terrible combats took place between them. The beast was driven further and further back toward the edge of the forest until it finally disappeared altogether, leaving the saintly hermit the conqueror. The places of their battles were marked by beds of beautiful lilies of the valley, which came up wherever the ground was sprinkled with the blood of the holy man. Every spring they appeared anew and the air around was filled with their fragrance. One of the emblems of the Virgin is a lily of the valley among thorns. Our Lady's tears is a name by which the flower is known.

FLOWER LORE AND LEGEND

For this reason, it was used, with other flowers, to decorate chapels, which were erected in honor of the Virgin. Being sometimes called the ladder to heaven, it is dedicated to Whitsuntide. As one of the blossoms that are supposed to belong peculiarly to St. George of England, it is also honored. In France, Germany, and Holland, lilies of the valley are known as mayflowers and in some parts of England they are called may lilies. Bishop Mant, in the Lily of the Valley, expresses very delicately the beauties of this little flower:

> "Fair flower, that, lapt in lowly glade,
> Dost hide beneath the greenwood shade,
> Than whom the vernal gale
> None fairer wakes, on bank, or spray,
> Old England's lily of the may,
> Our lily of the vale."

The leaves of the plant grow out from its creeping root and it is therefore known as a stemless plant, although its small, white, bell-shaped blossoms are attached to a stem.

> "Of thy twin leaves the embower'd screen
> Which wraps thee in thy shroud of green;
> Thy Eden-breathing smell,
> Thy arch'd and purple vestem stem,
> Whence pendent many a pearly gem,
> Displays a milk-white bell."

Grimm, the fairy story-teller, says that in some Hessian townships the holders of land have to pay a "bunch of mayflowers" (i.e. lilies of the valley) every year as rent. This custom had its origin in a religious ceremony, but is still observed out of respect to tradition. Great medicinal properties were attributed by the ancients to this plant. A delicious, perfumed liquid was distilled from the blossoms, which was

FLOWER LORE AND LEGEND

highly esteemed by the ancients as a remedy in nervous disorders. The liquid was regarded as of such value that it was kept only in bottles of silver and gold. It was also regarded as a cure for the gout. The old prescription read as follows: "Flowers of the lily of the valley being close stopped up in a glass, bury it in an ant hill for one month; taken out he shall find a liquid in the glass which, being outwardly applied, helpeth the gout."

Beauty doctors, who, in olden times, were called witches, used to prescribe its blossoms gathered before sunrise and rubbed on the face as a cure for freckles. In some counties in England the country people regard it as very unlucky to transplant a bed of these lilies, and the person who does so is expected to die within the twelvemonth. Although it is usually thought of as a white flower, there are several varieties, and the poets have taken note of this in some of their allusions. One has red blossoms, which Leigh Hunt refers to as "little illumination lamps"; while another has blossoms larger than the common sort, beautifully streaked with purple. Wordsworth, Keats, and Shelley make frequent allusions to this fairy flower, and all the English poets seem to have been familiar with it. Our own poets have not neglected it. Longfellow, Whittier, and Alice Cary have dedicated poems to its magic bells.

> "Innocent child and snow-white flower!
> Well are ye paired in your opening hour:
> Thus should the pure and the lovely meet,
> Stainless with stainless, and sweet with the sweet.
> White as those leaves just blown apart,
> Are the folds of thy own young heart,
> Guilty passion and cankering care,
> Never have left their traces there.
>
> William Cullen Bryant, The Children and the Lily.

FLOWER LORE AND LEGEND

THE VIOLET

CONSTANCY- MODESTY

"The violet in her greenwood bower,
Where birchen boughs with hazels mingle,
May boast herself the fairest flower,
In glen, or copse, or forest dingle."

Scott, The Violet.

The violet was dedicated to Orpheus and was under his especial protection, and it came about in this way:

When the god of music, with his lyre, charmed all the birds and the beasts, and even the rocks and the trees were moved by the strains, the flowers also came and danced around him. As exhausted, he sank upon a green bank to rest, his lyre dropped from his hand. On the spot where it fell sprang up the beautiful purple violet. There are a number of other legends associated with its origin. It seems to have been a favorite with the ancients. Almost every classic writer has had something to tell of the little flower. One mythological story is that Juno, who was very jealous of her husband, and with good reason, for Jupiter often neglected her, and was given to amusing himself with the nymphs, whenever he got a chance, was once very much surprised to have it turn dark suddenly, in the middle of the day. Her suspicions were immediately aroused. Brushing the dark cloud away as soon as possible, she saw Jupiter sitting quietly on the bank of a stream and near him a beautiful white heifer feeding. All around, instead of grass, the ground was covered with purple violets. She had her suspicions that it was some damsel whom Jupiter had transformed to deceive her, so she admired the animal and asked her husband to bestow it upon her as a gift. He could not well refuse his wife's request and consented. She had been correct in her conclusion. It was Io, the daughter of Inachus, the wind god, with whom Jupiter had been flirting, and whom he had changed into a heifer at the approach of his wife. Juno led poor Io a terrible life, until Mercury interceded for her, when, as Jupiter promised not to pay her any more attention, she was allowed to resume her own form and was restored to her parents. From this story is derived the Greek name of the violet, ion, because, wherever Io went, Jupiter caused these flowers to spring up for her to feed upon. The French poet, Rapin, gives another version of the origin of the flower. According to him, Midas, the King of Phrygia, had a beautiful daughter called Ianthis, who was betrothed to Atys.

Apollo saw her one day and was so delighted with her beauty that he demanded her in marriage. When her father, who hated him, refused to allow her to break with Atys, Apollo made up his mind to carry her off as Pluto did Proserpina. Ianthis was one of the maidens attendant upon Diana, and when the wicked sun-god seized her from his chariot, she called upon Diana to save her. The goddess, hearing her cry, changed her into a violet by the roadside. Hidden from sight, by her own green leaves, Apollo was forced to go away without her. Since then:

> "The violets have blossomed in the shade,
> Which their own leaves have made."

All violets are once said to have been white, but one variety became purple because Venus, sorrowing and forlorn, in seeking for Adonis, was impiously wounded on her foot by a thorn. The white violets in reverence and sympathy bowed their pallid heads and caught the drops of divine blood. Thus the original hue was tinged as if by purple dye. This story is retold in verse by Roscoe in Lorenzo de Medici:

FLOWER LORE AND LEGEND

> "Once Venus sorrowing, as all forlorn
> She sought Adonis, when a lurking thorn
> Deep on her foot impressed an impious wound,
> Then prone to earth we bowed our pallid flowers,
> And sought the drops divine, the purple dyes
> Tinging the luster of our native hue."

Clare refers the painters to the flower as Nature's pattern for the color, and reminds them of how impossible it will be to equal it:

> "Violets, sweet tenants of the shade,
> In purple's richest pride array'd,
> Your errand here fulfill;
> Go bid the artist's simple strain
> Your luster imitate in vain
> And match your Maker's skill."

It is an old saying that a handful of violets, not less, must be taken into the farmhouse each spring, as neglect of this ceremony brings destruction to the young chickens and ducks. In the days of the Pilgrims, violets were used as playthings. A hook is formed where the stem and the blossom unite. Children interlaced these hooks and by pulling tested their luck, as with a wishbone. The one who succeeded in pulling off the blossom from the stem held by another was declared the winner. Still another tale is given by Herrick, the English poet, who tells that the violets are descendants of some fair nymphs of whom Venus was jealous. One day she and Cupid had a dispute as to which was the sweetest.

> "And Venus having lost the day,
> Poore girls, she fell on you,
> And beat ye so, as some dare say
> Her blows did make ye blew."

FLOWER LORE AND LEGEND

Some writers have thought that the name was derived from the Latin word via, meaning road or way, as the violet is often spoken of as a wayside flower. It was a favorite with both the Greeks and the Romans. It was as much the national flower of the Athenians as the rose is of England, or the lily of France. It was cultivated in Athens and on sale in the markets at all seasons of the year, even when the snow was on the ground. A popular way of addressing the men of Athens was "Athenians crowned with violets."

The Romans, attributing medicinal qualities to it, were very much given to drinking a perfumed wine made from it. Pliny writes that a garland of violets, worn on the head, was a cure for headache and dizziness. Still later a paste made of violets and sugar was recommended for consumptives. It was also used for love philters. In Persia, the finest sherbet of the Mohammedans was flavored with violets. There is a tradition that Mohammed once said: "The excellence of the extract of violets, above all other extracts, is as the excellence of Me above all the rest of creation."

In England, in the olden times, the violet was regarded as an emblem of constancy. Ladies gave one to their knights to wear as a symbol of faithfulness. Our English forbears used to have a tradition that when roses and violets flourish late in the autumn it is a sign that a pestilence will ravage during the ensuing year. This was possibly the origin of the belief, which now exists, that a mild, damp winter is not as healthful as a colder season. There was an old saying, that: "A green Christmas maketh a fat graveyard."

At the floral games established by Clemence Isame, at Toulouse, in France, in 1323, the prize given to the writer of the best poem was a golden violet. These games are still celebrated there. They were discontinued during the French Revolution,

FLOWER LORE AND LEGEND

but were revived early in the nineteenth century.

When the first Napoleon left for Elba, it was said that he told his friends that he would return with the violets. During his absence, the flower was the secret badge of his adherents. They wore rings and watch-guards of violet color. As Corporal Violett, he was toasted and spoken of among his followers from the time he left France. On his return from exile, on the 20th of March, 1815 he was welcomed with showers of violets, which were then in full season. They continued to be the flower of the empire until after the battle of Waterloo, when it became dangerous to even be heard admiring them. No one dared even to wear one.

It was so generally recognized as the flower of the Bonapartes that it is said that Eugenie, afterwards the Empress, signified her acceptance of the suit of Napoleon III by appearing at a ball at the Tuileries wearing these flowers. Many years ago G. J. Clarke wrote the following lines for a little girl, dressed as a violet, to speak at a May-day festival:

> "Some plants, in gardens only found,
> Are raised with pains and care;
> God scatters violets all around,
> They blossom everywhere.
> Some scentless flowers stand straight and high,
> With pride and haughtiness,
> But violets perfume land and sky
> Although they promise less."

In literature, the poets of all ages and lands have sung its praises. Shakespeare's allusions to it are so many that some critics have felt justified in naming it as his favorite.
Byron has written some of his sweetest lines in praise of the 'little purple flower.' Keats often wrote of 'violet-beds nestling in sylvan bowers.'

FLOWER LORE AND LEGEND

Tennyson wrote of 'April violets,' Our own American poets have not neglected them. Bryant, Lowell, Whittier, the Cary sisters, and many others have found inspiration in them. B. W. Procter, better known as Barry Cornwall, the author of some of the sweetest songs of the last century, writes thus:

> "I love all things the seasons bring,
> All buds that start, all birds that sing,
> All leaves, from white to jet,
> All the sweet words that summer sends,
> When she recalls her flowery friends,
> But chief- the violet.
>
> She comes, the first, the fairest thing
> That heaven upon the earth doth fling,
> Ere Winter's star has set;
> She dwells behind her leafy screen,
> And gives, as angels give, unseen.
> So, love- the violet!
> Barry Cornwall, The Violet."

FLOWER LORE AND LEGEND

THE PANSY

HEARTSEASE - THOUGHTS

"Heartsease! One could look for half a day
Upon this flower, and shape in fancy out
Full twenty different tales of love and sorrow,
That gave the gentle name."

Mary Howitt.

"There is pansies, that's for thoughts."

Shakespeare, Hamlet.

The pansy is one of the oldest of garden flowers. Although it did not, as its sister violet, flourish in the garden of the gods, it is a flower of the people, and its cheapness and the ease with which it is cultivated have made it one of the most popular of plants. The name is a corruption of the French word pensees, meaning thoughts. Although the blossom is small, it has more and longer names than almost any other plant. In England alone, it has had at different times sixty distinct names, while in all Europe the number reaches to nearly two hundred. Among them the best known are heartsease, lady's delight, three-faces-under-a-hood, forget-me-not, love-in-idleness, cuddle-me-to-you, johnny-jump-up, kiss-me-at-the-garden-gate, and herb-trinity. Originally, as the story goes, it was of a milk-white color. One night, just before Midsummer Eve, the fairies had gathered to make preparations for their annual revel, and were discussing what they could do to make the world brighter for their being here. One little one timidly made a suggestion that they make a new flower. The rest were greatly pleased, and the very next night they went to work.

FLOWER LORE AND LEGEND

Getting out their paint boxes they took blue from the sky, different shades of red from the sunset clouds, yellow from the sunbeams, and a warm brown color from mother earth. These colors they mixed in a corn cup with their brushes made of dandelion down. All night they worked and when morning came there were the flowers gorgeously colored. Some of the fairies had sketched in portraits of their fellows, so that the bed of pansies looked like a bed of cheerful little faces. The earth has been brighter and better, ever since, for that night's work. There is another fairy story about the flower. Once there were some very foolish little sprites, who fell in love with some handsome youths, whom they met during one of their visits to the earth. They were young and did not realize that "fairies cannot with mortals mate." When their Queen heard of it she was very angry, and forbade them ever to leave fairyland again. The poor little things pined away and died, and Cupid felt so sorry for them that he persuaded the Queen to change them into the flower called heartsease, the juice of which:

> "On sleeping eyelids laid
> Will cause a man or woman to madly dote,
> Upon the next live creature that it sees."

Shakespeare has made use of this superstition in the Midsummer Night's Dream. In those days love philters were made from it. Another version of its origin is widely different from these. In a quaint, secluded spot there blossomed a little flower of exquisite coloring and fragrance. It was such a modest blossom that it had sought the most retired spot that it could find. A bird which was hopping about among the grasses saw it and flew away to tell the world of its beauty. An angel, coming down to earth on a mission of mercy, heard the bird singing of this vision of loveliness and asked to be conducted to it. When she saw the blossom, she cried: "Oh, thou art indeed lovely, too lovely to hide thus in the shade! Thou shalt go forth to gladden

FLOWER LORE AND LEGEND

the world with thy beauty and to scatter sweet thoughts throughout the earth." Then, sealing her blessing with a kiss, she passed on, leaving the impress of her face upon the flower. Thus the pansy went out into the world to be a joy to all who behold it. The touch of the angel had given it a perfume sweeter even than that of its sister, the violet. But while the violet grew by the wayside and in sheltered nooks, the pansy blossomed in the open fields. Seeking it, the people trampled down the grain and destroyed the crops. So the self-sacrificing little flower prayed to the Holy Trinity to take away its perfume, in order that it might not be so much sought after and that no more damage might be wrought on its account. The. request was granted.

The name Trinity-flower was given to the tenderhearted little blossom, in approval of its sacrifice. For centuries it was so known, and the name is not even yet obsolete in some parts of England. It is the flower used for Trinity Sunday. The curious construction of the pansy gives the imagination an opportunity to indulge in several quaint conceptions. In the center of every blossom lives a little old man, who, for punishment, must feel cold and be always wrapped up in a yellow blanket. He sits in the middle of the flower, with his feet in a foot tub, a queer little long narrow tub, so narrow that one wonders how he can get into it. If you will pick a pansy carefully apart you will see the little man, the little feet, and the little tub. In Scandinavia and Germany the flower is sometimes called the stepmother. This is the reason. There are five heart-shaped petals and behind these are five green sepals. The lower petal is the stepmother, and behind this are two of the sepals. The petals on each side of her are her own daughters with a sepal apiece, while the two upper leaves are her stepdaughters and one sepal does duty for both. The country folk therefore say that the stepmother takes two chairs and gives her daughters each a chair, while the two stepdaughters have both to sit on the same chair. Growing wild the colors of the flower are not as beautiful as when cultivated.

FLOWER LORE AND LEGEND

Children are very fond of it and many stories for them have been written about it.

> "The dear little pansies are lifting their heads,
> All purple and blue and gold.
> They're covering with beauty the garden beds,
> And hiding from sight the dull mold.
> Now all little children who try every day
> Kind-hearted and loving to be,
> Are helping the pansies to make the world bright,
> And beautiful, don't you see?"

The interesting formation of the flower was instrumental in turning the thoughts of Bartram, the first American botanist, to the study of that science. Bartram was a farmer and while directing his men at work in a field, on his farm in Delaware County, Pennsylvania, he picked a pansy that was growing at his feet. Thoughtlessly he pulled the flower apart and the somewhat grotesque formation of the blossom attracted his attention and aroused in his mind the interest in the habits and construction of plants, which made him an authority in his day and gained for him the friendship of the Swedish botanist, Linnaeus.

In the time of Shakespeare and Spenser it was certainly a familiar garden flower. Milton spoke of it as the "pansy streak'd with jet." Rapin, the French poet, called it "Jove's flower, in which three colors meet." Herrick pays a most graceful tribute to it as the "frolic virgins." The guide in Bunyan's Pilgrim's Progress called the attention of Christian and his sons to the shepherd boy singing to his sheep. "Do you hear him?" he says. "I will dare say that this boy leads a merrier life and wears more of that herb called heartsease in his bosom than he that is clothed in silk and purple." Leigh Hunt writes of the flower with "gratitude" as one of the friends who adorned his "prison house" and the one "which outlasted all the rest."

FLOWER LORE AND LEGEND

Writers for children, at the present time, find much in the pansy to emulate, and the plucky, cheerful little flower is frequently made use of to "point a moral and adorn a tale."

> "The flower, as nature's poet sweetly sings,
> Was once milk white, and heartsease was its name,
> Till wanton Cupid poised his roseate wings
> A vestal's sacred bosom to inflame,
> Heartsease no more the wandering shepherd found.
> No more the nymphs its snowy form possess;
> Its white now changed to purple by love's wound,
> Heartsease now, no more- 'tis love in idleness."

Mrs. Sheridan, Heartsease.

FLOWER LORE AND LEGEND

THE MIGNONETTE

YOUR QUALITIES SURPASS YOUR CHARMS

"Who gave you your name, Little Darling?
I wish that I knew,
Such a tiny, sweet, lovable blossom;
I half think that you grew
In the Garden of old, and believe
You were christened by Eve.
So whether in France or in Eden,
'Tis all one to me,
Yours is just the best name, Little Darling,
Could possibly be,
And though no one had taught me, I yet
Should say- Mignonette."

Susan Coolidge.

Lord Bacon, in his delectable essay on Gardens, says that because the breath of flowers is far sweeter in the air, "where it comes and goes like the warbling of music, than in the hand; therefore, nothing is more fit for that delight than to know something of the flowers that do best perfume the air." Among the simplest and sweetest-scented of these flowers is the fragrant mignonette. It is a native of Egypt, and among the ancients was known by the generic name of reseda, the meaning of which is "to assuage." In the days of the elder Pliny it grew luxuriantly near the city of Ariminum, now called Remini, in Italy, and was held in great esteem as a sedative for pain. It was also considered efficacious in reducing swellings and in allaying inflammation.

When used for the latter purpose, it was the custom to expectorate three times upon the ground, each time repeating

FLOWER LORE AND LEGEND

these words:

> "Reseda cause these maladies to cease,
> Knowest thou, knowest thou who has driven these pullets here?
> Let thy roots have neither head nor foot."

The flower was introduced into Southern France from Egypt about the middle of the eighteenth century, where it, at once, became very popular under the designation of mignonette, and this most appropriate name has clung to it ever since. It was not long before it became almost as popular in England and the London florists were kept busy supplying the window-boxes and balcony gardens of that city. One writer, describing London in 1790, writes that even in the lanes and alleys were seen small boxes and pots in which the fragrant plant was growing. One reason for its great popularity was the belief that it warded off certain diseases, which are carried through the air. Cowper, who was just twenty-one when the flower first made its appear6ance in London, made note of its popularity in The Task:

> "Sashes fronted with a range
> Of the fragrant herb, the Frenchman's darling."

In France, at the present time, the plant is cultivated in large quantities for use in the manufacture of perfumes. It is sometimes called dyer's rocket, on account of the resemblance of the leaves to a rocket and because it is made use of by dyers to color woolen stuffs yellow. Some botanists note the fact that the blossoms always follow the course of the sun, even upon a cloudy day, turning at sunrise toward the east, at noon toward the south, and in the evening facing the west. The following account of the origin of the flower is current among French children:

> There was once a young girl who was most unhappy

FLOWER LORE AND LEGEND

because she was so homely that she thought no one would ever love her. She shut herself up and wept most of the time. One day when she was feeling very sad, an old woman suddenly appeared and asked her why she was weeping. The maiden replied that she longed to be beautiful so that every one would love her. The fairy, for it was a fairy, said: "If you will do just as I tell you for one year, your wish will be granted. Go out into the world, and never let an hour pass without doing something to make someone happier, and do not look into a mirror until I come again." The old woman disappeared and where she had been standing was a plant growing in a flower-pot. The blossoms were insignificant, but the sweet odor filled the room. When the young girl saw it, she exclaimed: "Oh! the little darling." She put the plant carefully on the window-sill and started at once on her mission. She became so interested in helping people and in showing kindness to every one, old and young, who came in her way, that she forgot all about her looks, and the year passed so quickly that she hardly knew where it was gone. One day, when she was tending her plant, which had spread all over the window-garden, the fairy suddenly appeared again, and holding a mirror before the young girl, said, "Look." The girl could hardly believe that it was her own face that the glass reflected. Her eyes, which had been dim with weeping, were now bright and clear. Her cheeks were rosy and the whole expression of her face had changed. No one would dream of calling her even plain. The fairy smiled and said: "You have filled your heart with such beautiful thoughts and your life with such beautiful deeds that a beautiful soul shines in your face. Your wish is granted, and like the flower I left, you will create a sweet atmosphere about you wherever you go." The fairy disappeared and the flower has ever since been known as mignonette, which means little darling.

As herbe d'amour, or love-flower, it has been given a proud place in the armorial bearings of one of the noble families of Saxony. One of the Counts of Walsthim was betrothed to

FLOWER LORE AND LEGEND

Amelia von Nordbourg, a beautiful woman and an heiress, but also a coquette and very frivolous. As she was the only child of her widowed mother, her cousin Charlotte had been brought up with her from infancy as a companion. Charlotte, who was plain in appearance and had no dowry, received little attention in the gay circle of which her brilliant cousin was the center. One evening when a number of young people were gathered in the von Nordbourg drawing- room, it was suggested that each lady choose a flower, and the gentleman, to whom she should present it, must compose an appropriate verse. Charlotte, entering the room after most of the flowers had been selected, modestly chose a small sprig of mignonette. Amelia's choice had been the rose, and during the entire evening she had been receiving with evident pleasure the devoted attention of a dashing but rather disreputable colonel, to the evident annoyance of her betrothed. Charlotte, noticing the vexation of the nobleman, and desirous of recalling the wayward beauty to a sense of propriety, inquired what motto he had prepared for the rose. The Count saw through this affectionate ruse, and taking his pencil, wrote:

> "Its life is granted for a day,
> Its pleasures but a moment stay,"

which he handed to Amelia, at the same time presenting to Charlotte this line on the mignonette: "Its qualities surpass its charms." Amelia was so piqued at her lover's reproof that she carried her neglect too far and the count transferred his affections to her less attractive cousin. Upon his marriage to Charlotte he added a sprig of mignonette to his family arms, with the motto: "Your qualities surpass your charms." French writers of the latter part of the eighteenth and the early part of the nineteenth century paid much attention to the mignonette, and frequent reference is made to it by the English poets, although few poems are devoted exclusively to it. In descriptions of old gardens, particularly in Disraeli's works, it is given prominent mention. Perhaps one of

FLOWER LORE AND LEGEND

the most delicate tributes to the flower was paid by Bret Harte:

> "The delicate odor of mignonette,
> The ghost of a dead and gone bouquet,
> Is all that tells her story; yet,
> Could she think of a sweeter way?
>
> But whether she came as a sweet perfume,
> Or whether a spirit in stole of white,
> I feel as I pass from the darkened room,
> She has been with my soul tonight."

Bret Harte, Romance of Newport.

FLOWER LORE AND LEGEND

THE BUTTERCUP

RICHES - MEMORIES OF CHILDHOOD

"I never see a young hand hold
The starry bunch of green and gold,
But something warm and fresh will start
About the region of my heart."

Eliza Cook.

"The rich buttercup
Its tiny polished urn holds up,
Filled with ripe summer to the edge."

Lowell.

Buttercup is the pet name for the bright little flower which Thoreau, the 'Hermit of Walden,' has called the 'gold of the meadow.' The family name of the flower is crowfoot, which, like most surnames, had its origin in something especially appropriate to the object named, as the leaves of the plant are shaped something like a crow's foot. The botanical name of the flower is ranunculus, the diminutive of rana, which means frog, and was given to it in the very ancient times because it so often grew in places where the frogs sing. Another reason for giving it the name is beautifully told by Herrick, the English poet. Ranunculus was a Libyan youth, who was noted for his melodious voice and his gorgeous attire. He dressed altogether in green and yellow silk, and sang so sweetly that every one who heard him was charmed. He himself would often forget that any one was listening to him. One day when he was singing to a group of wood nymphs, he became so entranced with his own music that he expired in ecstasy and Orpheus transformed him

FLOWER LORE AND LEGEND

into the brilliant little flower that bears his name.

Tall crowfoot, one variety of buttercup, is supposed to be the plant referred to by Pliny as convivial, or the laughing leaves, which, when mixed with wine and myrrh and taken as a drink, caused strange visions to present themselves. It would excite the most inordinate laughter that often ended in death from convulsions. The only remedy he says for this singular condition was to dissolve pineapple kernels with pepper in wine from the date tree. It also has powerful caustic properties and it is said that if the leaves are bruised and applied to the skin, blisters, like those produced by the action of fire, will be raised. It was used by the ancients as a severe remedy in cases of leprosy and for removing birthmarks. Beggars sometimes resorted to it to produce sores upon their limbs to excite sympathy. The root was reputed to be a certain cure for insanity, if gathered at the wane of the moon, wrapped in a linen cloth, and suspended around the neck of the person affected. Feeding cattle avoid it. If they happen to get it, a blistered mouth is the result.

The Turks paid especial attention to its cultivation. Long before it was noticed in Europe, one of their viziers saw it growing among the grasses of the fields and caused it to be transplanted to the gardens of the seraglio, where it attracted the attention of the Sultan. He ordered as many varieties as possible to be planted there and carefully guarded. Through bribery, some specimens at last found their way into Europe. It is a social flower; shunning the gloom and shadow of the wood, flourishing only in the sunshine, and never thriving far from the habitation of men. No flower, except the daisy, is so closely associated with childhood. When Iris was made the messenger for the gods, the sun and the ocean built a bridge for her of beautiful colors like the rainbow. One end rested in the sky and the other was fastened to the earth by a large bag of gold. Many had started in quest of this gold, but no one had ever succeeded in finding it. At last a little boy heard of it, and determining to make it the main object of his life to secure this treasure, he left everything, father, mother, home, friends, and started on his long journey. For many years he traveled, but seemed to get no nearer to his goal. One night after he had lain down to rest, worn out with a long day of travel, a beautiful lady in shining white robes appeared to him, and holding up a mirror, said: "Behold!" He looked and instead of the innocent boy who had started on the long quest, he saw an old man, worn, gray, and wrinkled. The shining lady looked at him sadly and said: "You will attain the object of your search, but, as you have never turned aside to give pleasure to others, or to succor those in distress, so your wealth will bring you no happiness." She disappeared, and when he arose he found himself standing on the brow of a cliff overlooking a deep valley. There had been a gentle shower, the sun shone through the raindrops, and the beautiful bridge seemed to end in the valley at his feet. The old man clambered down the hillside, and where the end of the rainbow apparently touched the earth he found his long-sought treasure. Afraid that if any one knew of his wealth they might ask for some of it, he determined to hide it in the earth. Waiting until it was dark, he took the bag on his back and stole carefully along beside the brook and through the meadow in search of a good place to secrete his gold. The fairies were holding a conservation congress in that very meadow to decide the best way to preserve to the world kindness, unselfishness, and happiness. As the old man crept along an elf stepped up behind him, and, with a sharp blade of grass, cut a small hole in his bag. One by one the pieces of yellow gold dropped out and lay among the grass. When the old man reached his destination his bag was empty, but all along behind him sparkled the gold pieces he had dropped. One of the fairies suggested that they fasten stems to them, so that they might not sink into the ground. All night long the little people worked, and when the sun rose in the morning, the grassy meadow was sprinkled with beautiful yellow flowers, clear down to the side of the brook. When the

FLOWER LORE AND LEGEND

children wondered how they came there, the fairies smiled to themselves, for they knew all about it, while the old man was so angry, when he found his treasure gone, that he quickly disappeared, and no one ever saw him again.

The buttercups have been blooming ever since. Children still hold them under the chin to test their fondness for butter, as they search for the gold at the end of the rainbow, while near by the little frogs almost burst with their own music. Quite an extensive bibliography might be made on the buttercup and while a large proportion would be classed under children their elders would find much that is interesting. Thoreau, Higginson, and John Burroughs have all moralized over the cheerful little flower. Dr. Hugh McMillan, of Glasgow, has written a wonderful chapter on the "flower of the buttercup." Under the name of king's cup, great English writers have made many references to it, but most of the poets, grave and gay, agree with Browning that it is "the children's dower" and all seem to find it redolent with "memories of childhood."

> "I pluck the flowers I plucked of old
> About my feet- yet fresh and cold,
> The buttercups do bend;
> The self-same buttercups they seem,
> All in their bright-eyed green, and such
> As when to me their blissful gleam
> Was all earth's gold- how much?"

Owen Meredith.

FLOWER LORE AND LEGEND

THE FORGET-ME-NOT

REMEMBRANCE

"Pray tell me, sweet forget-me-not,
Oh, kindly tell me where you got
Your curious name?
I'm most desirous to be told
The legend or romance of old
From whence it came."

Oliver Herford.

Myosotis is the family name of the little blue flower that we know as forget-me-not. In almost every European language it bears a name with the same meaning, and each nation has its own tradition as to the origin of the meaning. The one that takes precedence by reason of its antiquity is credited to the East. When Adam gave names to all the flowers in the Garden of Eden, he cautioned them to be careful not to forget their names. One little blue flower was inattentive and had to go back to the gardener to ask him the name which he had given it. The first school-master looked down kindly on the poor little frightened blossom and said, 'Forget- not.' Ever since it has borne that name.

The Greeks tell us that in the golden age of the early world a messenger of Jupiter fell in love with a mortal maiden and in consequence was shut out of Paradise. He sat outside the gate weeping until Jove, taking pity on him, gave him a quantity of seed, and told him that when they had planted it beside every brook and pool in every corner of the world he would admit them to his presence. The messenger and his loved one wandered up and down the face of the earth for years, and when their task

FLOWER LORE AND LEGEND

was finished the gates opened and they were admitted to the heaven of the gods. The maiden was permitted to become immortal without tasting the pangs of death, because of the service she had assisted in rendering to mortals. After the gates had closed upon them, wherever they had planted the seed the forget-me-not sprang up, and it is still a perpetual reminder of their faithfulness to each other and to their work.

In Germany there is an element of tragedy connected with the name of the flower, which appeals to all young people. A knight and his lady-love, on the eve of their marriage, while walking on the banks of the Danube, saw a spray of beautiful blue flowers which the water had dislodged and was about to carry down the stream. She expressed a wish for them and her lover, plunging into the water, grasped the flowers, but the current was too strong for him. As it carried him past the weeping maid he threw the flowers on the bank saying, as he was swept on toward the sea, 'Vergissrneinnicht' which means forget me not, and by that name the flower has ever since been known. Mills, in the History of Chivalry, tells the tale. A verse about the occurrence is translated thus:

> "And the lady fair, of the knight so true,
> Ay remembered his hopeless lot,
> And she cherished the flower of brilliant hue,
> And braided her hair with the blossoms blue,
> And she called it forget-me-not."

It is related that the Princess Marie and Napoleon were once walking by the Rhine, when the wind blew a flower from her hair into the water. With the legend in mind she exclaimed, "What a chance for a knight of the olden time!" Napoleon immediately sprang into the water after it, but on reaching shore, nearly drowned, said to her, "Take it, Marie, but never again speak to me of an ancient knight." In Teutonic fairy tales it is

FLOWER LORE AND LEGEND

classed with the luck or key-flowers, which have the magical power of opening mountain sides or subterranean caverns and disclosing treasure. Grimm, the fairy story-teller, makes use of this quality of the flower in several of his stories. One of them tells of a shepherd, who, while wandering over a mountain, picked a sprig of blue flower and placed it in his hat band. Immediately a door in the side of the hill opened and the man entered a passage which led into a beautiful room filled with gold and precious stones.

In his eagerness to carry away as much as possible of the treasure he took off his hat to use as a receptacle and the key-flower dropped to the ground. As he turned to leave the cavern a faint voice called to him, "Forget not the best." He went back and selected several more of the finest jewels, but he never thought of the little flower that he had gathered on the mountain side. As he passed through the opening the mountain closed and crushed him to death. The exact counterpart of the flower, as it grows in the Alps, in Switzerland, has been found on Mount Holmes, in the National Yellowstone Park, in Montana. It is botanically known as myosotis alpestris.

The forget-me-not, like the red-and-white rose, had its place in English history. When Henry of Lancaster was banished by Richard, he chose it for his emblem and the words, "Couveigne vous de moi," as his motto. They were woven into his knight's collar. His adherents, following his example, wore forget-me-nots as an evidence of their fidelity. One of these collars, made of gold with the flowers and motto enameled in blue, was given as a prize at a famous tournament, during the reign of Edward IV. It was won by Lord Scales, the brother of the Queen. More than one historian is authority for the fact that after the battle of Waterloo an immense quantity of forget-me-nots sprang up in different parts of the battlefield.

FLOWER LORE AND LEGEND

The Italians tell of a beautiful maiden who was beloved of the gods, and when she was drowned they transformed her into the blue forget-me-not, growing on the river bank. The name myosotis is derived from the Greek and signifies mouse-ear, because of the shape of the leaves. Another name by which the plant used to be called was scorpion grass, perhaps on account of the spike resembling the tail of a scorpion. It was popularly supposed to be a cure for the bite of that animal. Many flowers are assigned as appropriate to particular days. The day of the forget-me-not is February 29th.

In England, France, and the Netherlands, about the Middle Ages, the name forget-me-not was given to the ground pine on account of the bitter taste it leaves in the mouth, and in some parts of England it used to be called speed-well, because when the blossoms fell off they blew away. The name which was perpetuated by the ship that came to New England in the time of the Pilgrims is an ancient form of bidding farewell or good-by. There is hardly a poet who has not, at some time or other, taken the forget-me-not as a theme. Most of them use it in a sentimental fashion, but not all. Goethe calls it "still the liveliest flower, the fairest of the fair."

Coleridge writes: "Hope's gentle gem, the sweet forget-me-not." Longfellow called the stars "the forget-me-nots of the angels," and Eugene Field tells of the "solace and peace of forget-me-not." One poet pays this tribute to the little blue flower:

> "Of all the flowers that deck the field,
> Or grace the garden of the heart,
> Though others richer perfume yield,
> The sweetest is forget-me-not."

Anonymous.

FLOWER LORE AND LEGEND

THE HYACINTH

SPORT – GAME - PLAY

"And the hyacinth purple, and white, and blue,
Which flung from its bells a sweet peal anew,
Of music so delicate, soft, and intense,
It was felt like an odor within the sense."

Shelley.

Apollo, the god of music, was devoted to a Laconian youth, named Hyacinthus. He loved him so much that he was unhappy when they were not together. As companions, they hunted, fished, roamed the forest, and played games.

One day, as they were throwing quoits, Apollo, pitching with great strength, sent the discus with much force through the air. Hyacinthus, excited, ran forward eager to meet his throw. The quoit swerved and hit him in the forehead. He fell to the earth, and Apollo, heart-broken at the sight of his pale face and flowing blood, tried every art to restore him to consciousness, but in vain. Weeping over his dead friend, he said: "Thy death is at my door; would that I could die for thee, but since that cannot be, my lyre shall keep thy memory alive, my song shall tell thy fate."

When he had finished speaking, lo!- the blood which had stained the sod was blood no longer. A beautiful flower had sprung up, the stalk of which was hung with lovely purple bells. This flower will forever bear the name of Hyacinthus, and each spring revive his memory. Zephyr, the west wind, also loved him and was very jealous of his affection for Apollo. It was said by some of those who were watching the game that he puffed the discus out of its course, unintentionally causing the blow. An annual celebration was established in Laconia to commemorate the event. It lasted three days, during which the people ate no bread, but lived entirely on sweets and refrained from wearing garlands in their hair. On the second day a company of youths entertained the public by playing on the harp and flute and singing choruses to Apollo. Others appeared upon richly caparisoned horses, singing country folk-songs, while the throng who accompanied them danced to the music. Beautiful maidens, magnificently appareled, rode in canopied wagons drawn by bullocks, and sang hymns. Some took part in chariot races.

Many victims were sacrificed to the sun-god and the worshipers were lavish in their hospitality. There has been much discussion in regard to the hyacinth, and the claim of the modern flower to be the blossom which sprung from the blood of Hyacinthus has been disputed. By some it is asserted that the martagon lily, or Turk's cap, was the plant referred to by the poet Ovid, who tells the story. This is probably correct as the common hyacinth has neither the blood color nor the marks which resemble the Greek 'ai, 'ai, meaning alas, the cry which the storied legend requires. These marks are only found upon the Turk's cap. Claims have also been made in behalf of the gladiolus and the larkspur. Homer mentions the hyacinth as among the flowers that decked the couch of Jupiter. Poets often describe curly hair as "hyacinthine locks": the tightly curled leaves of the flower being representative of the hair of Hyacinthus, which was very curly. Leigh Hunt, in his Songs and Chorus of the Flowers, said:

"Drooping grace unfurls
Still Hyacinthus curls."

In the Grecian isles the bridal wreaths were made of hyacinths and crowns of the blossom were worn by the maidens who attended the bride.

Curiously, this flower is also associated with death. The emanations from it are reputed to be very poisonous when inhaled in large quantity. In France is recorded a murder which was said to have been accomplished by filling the room of the victim with hyacinths while he was sleeping. In Holland the plant is the pride of the Dutch florists. Although the craze for it never reached the extent of the tulip mania, it has been and still is a great source of wealth. In 1890 a tract of land equal to a thousand English acres was in use for cultivating the bulbs, and it was estimated that nearly forty thousand persons were directly dependent on the trade for their livelihood. The credit for having produced the first double hyacinth is given to Peter Voerhelm, a florist of Harlem. For one bulb he is said to have received a thousand pounds sterling. He called it the King of Great Britain, and it is considered the oldest double variety in existence. From the time of the ancients until the present day we find many allusions to the flower in literature. Milton, Byron, Burns, and Collins have each given it a place in verse. Burns makes it an emblem of fidelity. "The hyacinth for constancy wi' its unchanging blue." The common variety is often called the harebell by poetical writers, and under that name has received countless poetical tributes, although its right to retain them is now contested. The purple blossom which sprung from the blood of Hyacinthus is emblematic of the sorrowful and sad:

> "The melancholy hyacinth that weeps all night,
> And never lifts an eye all day.
> The white one represents unobtrusive loveliness:
> The daintiest flowers that were ever seen,
>
> Each a pearly bell.
> Hidden so well that no one could guess,
> From the bulb in the earth,

FLOWER LORE AND LEGEND

What an exquisite angel of loveliness

Was waiting for birth.
Then some day, lovely as a queen
From fairyland,
All snowy white, 'twixt leaves of green
My flower will stand!"

Mary E. Atkinson, The Hyacinth.

FLOWER LORE AND LEGEND

THE MARGUERITE. A DAISY

INNOCENCE

"There is a flower, a little flower,
With silver crest and golden eye:
That welcomes every changing hour,
And weathers every sky."

Montgomery, The Daisy.

"We meet thee like a pleasant thought."

Wordsworth, To a Daisy.

According to the classic legend, it owes its origin to Bellis, a dryad or nymph of the wood, who was one of the granddaughters of Danseus and the betrothed of Epigeus. One day when she was dancing with him she attracted the attention of Vertumnus, the deity of fruit trees. Determining to marry her, in spite of Epigeus, and that she might be concealed from him, he changed her into a flower which in the scientific world bears her name.

Some writers have dedicated the daisy to infancy as the flower of innocence, and the Celtic version of its origin is their authority. The story is found in the poems of Ossian, a mythical bard of Ireland. Malvina, the daughter of Toscar of Lutha, when her infant son was taken from her, was inconsolable, and, while she was bemoaning her loss, the maidens of the court of the King of Morven came to her and told her that they had seen her beautiful boy approaching them in a light mist, looking radiantly happy and dropping over the fields a new flower with a golden disk, which was surrounded by silver leaves like the rays of the

FLOWER LORE AND LEGEND

sun. As the blossoms stirred gently in the breeze they looked like infants playing in a green meadow. The maidens called the flower the 'day's-eye,' because it closed at night and opened with the first beam of day. Its German name means meadow pearl, while in France it is marguerite, which also means pearl. It is not always the rarest or most expensive flower that takes the most prominent place in history.

Margaret of Anjou, the unhappy wife of Henry VI of England, when a little girl, chose the marguerite for her emblem, and when she came to England all the nobles of the court and their wives and daughters wore daisies to welcome the French bride. The King had her emblem flower engraved on all his plate. Margaret, the sister whom Francis I loved so dearly that he called her the 'Marguerite of marguerites,' and also her daughter Margaret, chose this flower for their own. When the latter was married, she was presented with a basket of daisies accompanied by the sentiment : "All flowers have charms, but though I had the choice of a thousand, I should choose the marguerite."

Philip the Bald, of Burgundy, instituted an 'order of the daisy' in honor of his wife, Margaret of Flanders. Louis IX, called St. Louis, who married a Margaret, had a daisy engraved on his signet-ring together with a cross and a lily, which he said stood for all that he held, dear, religion, France, and love. Margaret of Richmond, mother of Henry VII, used as her device three daisies on a green field. In 1868, when Prince Humbert, the first king of United Italy, married Margaret of Savoy, the people celebrated the event by wearing wreaths and bouquets of the name flower of the Princess, and among her wedding gifts was a necklace from Victor Emmanuel made of gold and pearls set as marguerites.

The flower was especially regarded as belonging to young maidens, and was used by them as an oracle to test the

FLOWER LORE AND LEGEND

fidelity of their lovers. Goethe uses this superstition with wonderful effect in the scene between Marguerite and Faust. The roots of the plant placed under the pillow were supposed to induce pleasant dreams of absent loved ones, but while in the spring it was considered fortunate to dream of daisies, in the winter it was most unlucky. For years a charming feature of class-day at Vassar has been that in which the daisy plays a prominent part. The college is surrounded by fields, which at commencement time are white with the flower. The sophomore classes gather them and weave them into a chain, which is sometimes one hundred and eighty feet long. At the planting of the senior class tree, twenty-four girls, who have been selected by vote as the handsomest girls in the class, wearing white gowns, precede the seniors, carrying the daisy-chain fastened from their shoulders.

It is no light task, for the chain is very heavy; sometimes each girl sustains as much as twenty pounds in weight. At the commencement in it was decided to abandon this beautiful ceremonial, because, it is said, the choice of the twenty-four most beautiful maidens has deteriorated into a 'beauty contest,' which occasions hard feeling not becoming to the dignity of an institution of learning. If the maids were merely selected by lot the custom which has meant so much to the institution might still go on. In 19 17 the vote was in favor of restoring the daisy chain. A similar custom exists at Bradford Academy, Bradford, Mass. Younger girls also play with the daisies. The yellow disks, when the petals are gone, make pumpkin pies for the doll's table. By clipping off the rays to shape a cap and leaving two long ones for strings, with a little ink, a capped grandmother's head and face are made. In literature the daisy has a place only second to the rose. It was a favorite with Chaucer, who says of all flowers he loves it the most, and in the Legend of Good Women he tells of Queen Alceste, who was changed into an 'ee of the Daie,' each leaf representing one of her virtues. Ben Jonson and Dryden both write of it in glowing measures. Shakespeare names it among the flowers of poor Ophelia's fatal garland. Dante, in one of his visions of Paradise, sees it as one of the flowers of the blessed, with its face ever turned toward God.

Readers of Goethe and Schiller are familiar with their treatment of the little 'oracle' and later writers have not neglected to sing its praises. Keats, when dying, said he could already feel daisies growing on his grave. In church circles, it is the flower of St. Margaret of the Dragon, whose special day is June 20th, when the blossoms are at their best. Soon after St. Augustine came to England he saw a field covered with them. Overcome by the sight, falling on his knees, he exclaimed; "Behold! a hundred pearls, so will the spirits of the blest shine in heaven." Once when he was about to speak to a large audience, out of doors, he observed a boy wearing a daisy chain. Taking it, he pulled the flowers slowly apart before the crowd as he preached his great sermon on Christian brotherhood.

"The sun," he said, "has imaged himself in the center of each of these flowers, as the Sun of Righteousness will image Himself in each of your hearts. From this sun in the daisy white rays spread round. So may the rays of purity and goodness spread around you, reflected from the light of heaven within you. As these flowers are strung together in a chain, so may you in England be united to each other, and to the holy churches of the world, by a chain that shall never be broken. Unlike the feeble stems of these daisies, that a child's fingers can sever, may the links of your chain be indissolubly connected, not to be broken, though strained and divided in ages to come, until the great Creator of your being shall bring you all safe into His everlasting kingdom."

Great honors were paid to the daisy by Chaucer and the old English poets:

FLOWER LORE AND LEGEND

"Daisies, ye flowers of lowly birth,
Embroiderers of the carpet earth,
That stud the velvet sod;
Open to spring's refreshing air,
In sweetest smiling bloom declare
Your Maker and my God.
Clare, Bowing Adorers."

FLOWER LORE AND LEGEND

THE PEONY

BASHFULNESS

"Erect in all her crimson pomp you'll see
With bushy leaves the graceful peony."

Rapin.

Aesculapius was the son of Apollo, and while still an infant was entrusted to the care of Chiron, the wisest and most just of all the centaurs. He bestowed upon the youth much care and instructed him so thoroughly in the art of healing that when he was grown he was renowned for his skill and knowledge and was known as the paeon, or helper, and was the first physician of the gods. One day Hippolytus was killed by a fall from his chariot and Paeon, with his knowledge and skill, restored him to life. This so alarmed Pluto, the king of the infernal regions, that he persuaded Jupiter to annihilate Aesculapius with one of his terrible thunderbolts.

Apollo was so grieved by the death of his son that Jove took pity on him, and instead of giving the body of Aesculapius into the keeping of Pluto, he transformed it into a peony, perpetuating the name by which he was best known among the gods. It is said to have been the first plant used for medical purposes. As Homer tells the tale, it differs somewhat from other ancient versions. According to his story, Pluto had been severely wounded by Hercules, and Paeon cured him by means of a plant which he received from his grandmother, the mother of Apollo. In gratitude, Pluto caused the plant to be called paeonia, to honor the memory of the great physician of Mount Olympus. Another account of the origin of the plant is that Paeonia was a beautiful nymph. One day Apollo, who was not always discreet, was indulging in a mild flirtation with her. Paeonia happening to turn her head saw Venus regarding her with great severity. She blushed so red that the color never left her face, and when Venus in her anger changed her into a flower she still retained the rosy hue. The Greeks held it in great reverence as a sacred flower. They believed that it was an emanation from the moon, and was under the especial protection of that planet; that the flower was illuminated during the night, driving away evil spirits and protecting those who cultivated it. A small piece of the root, worn as an amulet around the neck, was thought to be a sure protection from evil enchantments. The healing properties of the plant, though not as numerous as those of some others, were said to be unfailing. The root boiled in water was a certain cure for intestinal affections. Boiled in wine it was used for diseases of the stomach. Fifteen black seeds eaten before retiring were thought to prevent nightmare. As late as the sixteenth century beads were made from the roots and worn by children as a safeguard against convulsions. One writer in the second century assures us that the extract was efficacious in cases of insanity. Pliny classes the plant as a cure for falling sickness. Other ancient writers claim that worn as an amulet the flower will prevent enchantment. Block says it was one of the 'old folke' medicines. All early writers agree that the roots must be taken up with great care after dark, as the plant is carefully guarded by Picus, the woodpecker of Mars, who would attack the eyes of any one attempting to disturb the plant. In China, as the queen flower, it is called man-tan-fa, and is regarded with reverence and pride, being cultivated very carefully. The great tree peony, the triumph of the Chinese flower-world, grows to a height of eight feet. Some of the blossoms are of enormous size, measuring nine inches across. On the bush peony they are frequently so large and heavy as to require artificial support. The Chinese name means flower of prosperity. It is also called the plant of twenty days, because it is said that the blossoms retain their beauty and freshness for that length of time. The flower is

FLOWER LORE AND LEGEND

used extensively in Chinese art and decoration. In connection with the peacock, it is a favorite subject for temple and palace walls. In this country it has been considered as an old fashioned flower, a survival of the 'good old colony times,' when no New England front yard was complete without its 'piny bush.' As it is a hardy perennial, there are still in some New England gardens peony plants almost as old as the homesteads themselves, that have been known to have had one hundred blossoms at a time. In poetry it has been strangely neglected. Shakespeare, in the Tempest, makes Iris speak of the meadows 'with their pionied and lilied banks,' and one or two of the very early English writers mention it, spelling the name in various ways. One writer, in the sixteenth century, tells of a garden;

> "With gilly flowers all set round,
> And pyonys powdered ay betwene."

Of the later poets, Jean Ingelow writes of the leaves:

"At the roots
Of the peony bushes in rose-red heaps
Or snowy fallen blooms."

But it is in stories of colonial life that the peony shines. Dr. Oliver Wendell Holmes called it 'an aristocratic flower,' while Mary E. Wilkins has honored it by giving its name to one of her stories. The variety known as moutans has flourished and been highly regarded in China for fifteen hundred years. In England it begins to bloom in April, but in this country it is later. Thy banks with pionied and lilied brims,

> "Which spongy April at the best betrims
> To make cold nymphs chaste crowns."
> Shakespeare, The Tempest.

FLOWER LORE AND LEGEND

THE SUNFLOWER

CONSTANCY - ADORATION

"Ah, sunflower, weary of time,
Who countest the steps of the sun:
Seeking after that sweet golden clime,
When the traveler's journey is done."

William Blake.

"Miles and miles of golden green,
Where the sunflowers blow,
In a solid glow."

Robert Browning.

The helianthus, or old-fashioned sunflower, is associated in the minds of almost every one with the ancient myth of Clytie and Apollo, as related by Ovid. The name is derived from Helios, the sun, and anthos, a flower, and there is no doubt that the sunflower in the minds of the Greeks bore a resemblance to the orb of the day. Some writers have endeavored to demonstrate that the heliotrope (one of the flowers sacred to the sun) was unknown to the ancients, so in lack of definite information the common mind has accepted, if not the sunflower of the present day, at least one of the same species as the subject of the legend.

One of the most familiar pieces of old sculptures discovered in modern times is the bust now in the British Museum and frequently reproduced, generally known as Clytie. The name was arbitrarily given to it because it rises from the leaves of a large blossom, which it does not require a vivid imagination to accept as a sunflower. Clytie was a beautiful

FLOWER LORE AND LEGEND

water-nymph, the daughter of Oceanus. One day she left her home among the waves and the sea flowers and joined the assembly of the gods on Mount Olympus. There she saw Apollo, the sun-god, in all his glory, and, foolish little nymph, fell desperately in love with him. Apollo was just then very much enamored of Calliope, the muse of epic poetry, and paid no attention to Clytie. So she pined away, sitting all day long upon the cold ground, with her hair streaming on her shoulders, gazing upon the sun from the time he appeared in the morning until he sank behind the horizon. For nine days she sat there, tasting neither food nor drink, and resisting all entreaties of the other water-nymphs to return to her home in the sea. At last her limbs sank into the earth and became roots, her body changed into a long, slender stem, and her beautiful face was transformed into a flower, which reflected the rays of the sun and turned toward him all day in his course through the heavens. When the old-time Spanish invaders arrived in Peru they found that the worship of the sun still prevailed among the inhabitants and that the sunflower was much reverenced on account of its resemblance. They described the Temple of the Sun as ornamented with representations of the sun made of the purest gold and of exquisite workmanship.

The priestesses were crowned with sunflowers and wore them on their bosoms and carried them in their hands. Some of the travelers called the plant the Indian sonne-fleur; others the golden flower of Peru. It was introduced at that time into Spain. Within the next twenty years we find references made to the sunflower gardens of Madrid. As a symbol of constancy and devotion it has its place in the Christian religion. Being the flower of light and sunshine, it is dedicated to St. John the Evangelist. A window in the Church of St. Remi, at Rheims, represents the Holy Mother and St. John on either side of the Cross. The head of each is encircled by an aureole of sunflowers, all turned toward the Savior as to the true sun. An anonymous

FLOWER LORE AND LEGEND

writer, in an ode to the sunflower, embodied this:

> "Emblem of constancy, whilst he is beaming,
> For whom is thy passion so steadfast, so true;
> May we, who of faith and of love are aye dreaming,
> Be taught to remember this lesson by you."

It is the especial emblem of St. Bartholomew. An old rhyming calendar written about the fifteenth century thus notes this fact:

> "And yet anon the full sunflower flew,
> And became a starre for Bartholomew."

In 1 615, when Champlain explored the Georgian Bay region, he noted the fact that the Indians were cultivating it and using the seeds for food, procuring from them also an oil for their hair. It has assumed a remarkable economic important in Russia. It is said that the land devoted to it yields twice as much in money value as that producing any other crop. The finer quality of seed is used for food and is regarded as a great delicacy by all classes. From the second quality an oil is made, the best grades of which are extremely nutritious and as delicate in flavor and color as the best salad oils of culinary and domestic purposes in Russia and on the continent. The oil cake is used for fodder for horses and cattle. The stalks of the plant make a fuel resembling pine. They burn quickly and produce a bright, fragrant fire. Even the ashes have a commercial value for fertilizing purposes. In China the plant is being grown extensively. A beautiful silk fabric is made from the fiber of the stalks. Italy and India, also, are learning its commercial value.

Hyll, in the Art of Gardening, which was printed in 1586, says that it was so called... "for that after the rising of the sun unto noon this flower openeth larger and larger; but after

FLOWER LORE AND LEGEND

the noon-time unto the setting of the sun the flower closeth more and more, so that after the setting thereof, it is wholly shut up."

Thompson says:

"The lofty follower of the sun
Sad, when he sets, shuts up her yellow leaves
Drooping all night, and, when he warm returns,
Points her enamour'd bosom to his ray."

For many years in America and England the decorative qualities of the sunflower were not appreciated, and it was relegated to the kitchen garden; but with the advent of the pre-Raphaelites the plant as a whole was suddenly given what was by many regarded as undue prominence. In the early 80s of the last century it obtained a place in decorative art, which it has never lost. In Gilbert and Sullivan's opera of Patience, it was a 'leading lady' and was more or less associated with the unfortunate Oscar Wilde.

It grows so prolifically in this country that it has been suggested as the national flower. It is a native of every state in the Union. The wild is much smaller than the cultivated variety. In some of the western states, in August and September, the railroads are lined on either side with millions of the yellow blossoms, all turning their faces to follow the course of the sun. Kansas and Nebraska have chosen it as the state flower. Lately its economic value has been recognized and in 1901 Dr. Harvey W. Wiley, under the direction of the department of agriculture, issued a bulletin devoted to its cultivation, composition, and uses. In this bulletin, among the other properties of the plant, it is noted that the seeds are in demand for keeping horses and cattle in excellent physical condition. The attention is also called to it as a preventive of malaria.

FLOWER LORE AND LEGEND

Although the sunflower has been regarded as common, the poets have considered it worthy of their best efforts. Calderon, the Spanish poet, to whom the gardens of Madrid were probably a familiar sight, thus addresses it:

> "Sight enchanted sunflower, thou
> Who gazest ever true and tender
> On the sun's revolving splendor."

Erasmus Darwin, grandfather of the great Darwin, and himself a naturalist and a poet, in his Loves of the Plants, writes thus:

> "With zealous steps, he climbs the upland lawn
> And bows in homage to the rising dawn.
> Imbibes with eagle eye, the golden ray,
> And watches as it moves, the orb of day."

But of all the tributes, the one appealing most to the universal heart and that will never be forgotten as long as there are voices to sing and hearts to feel, is:

> "The heart which has truly loved never forgets,
> But as truly loves on to the close,
> As the sunflower turns on her god when he sets,
> The same look which she turned when he rose."

Thomas Moore.

FLOWER LORE AND LEGEND

THE CLOVER

I PROMISE

"Sweet by the roadsides, sweet by the rills,
Sweet in the meadows, sweet on the hills,
Sweet in its white, sweet in its red-
Oh, half of its sweetness cannot be said;
Sweet in its every living breath,
Sweetest, perhaps, at last in death."

Saxe Holm, Song of the Clover.

"There is music at our feet,
On the clover, honey sweet.

Walter Thornbury."

While there is no authenticated myth as to the origin of the clover, it is certain that the ancients held it in great favor. Hope is represented as a child standing on tiptoe and holding out clover blossoms. Summer bestows clover as a promise of future good. The Greeks used it extensively for garlands and in decorations for their festivals. It was introduced into Greece, says Pliny, from Media during the reign of Darius, the Persian. The generic name of the plant is tri folium, meaning one leaf with three parts. The latest authorities give three hundred varieties. The Druids, an ancient order of Celtic priests, whose name is derived from a word meaning tree, regarded it as one of their sacred plants and held it in a veneration second only to the mistletoe. The name comes from clava, a Celtic word for club. Some say that the little three-part leaf is supposed to have been given its name from its resemblance to the three-headed club of the great Hercules.

FLOWER LORE AND LEGEND

But interest in the clover chiefly centers in the fact that it is the national floral emblem of the Emerald Isle. In the early days of the mission of the great St. Patrick, he was preaching one day in the neighborhood of Meath, and was endeavoring to explain the doctrine of the Trinity to an audience who found it difficult to comprehend. "How," asked one of the chiefs, "can there be three in one?" The Saint stopped and picked from the sod at his feet a clover leaf. Holding it before them he said: "Behold, in this trifoliate leaf, how three persons in the Godhead can exist, and yet be one." The illustration was so familiar and yet so forcible that the chief and his whole clan accepted the Christian faith. From this tradition in all probability came the adoption in later years of the shamrock as the national emblem. There has been some conflict as to whether the wood-sorrel, or the white clover, was the original shamrock of Ireland.

Decision has been generally in favor of the clover. As the trefoil is the emblem of the Trinity, it is used in decoration for Trinity Sunday. The early Christians imagined that the stem represented the path of life, the right-hand leaf purgatory, the left-hand hades, and the center heaven. Still another interpretation was that the threefold leaf was an emblem of faith, hope, and love, the three great elements in Christian life. Consequently it has been introduced as a feature of ecclesiastical architecture. The extremities of crosses and church windows, as well as interior and exterior decorations, are often made in its form. The clover is one of the plants that undergo a radical change at night. As evening comes on, the side leaves fold together, while the center leaf bends over them in a prayerful attitude. This transformation was no doubt an additional reason for the reverence with which the plant was cherished. Perhaps it will account for the idea which prevailed that it was antagonistic to evil spirits and counteracted their influence. The various kinds always contract at the approach of a storm, and hence it is known as the husbandman's barometer. The leaves rise up to protect the

FLOWER LORE AND LEGEND

blossom. In some places it was believed that if a farmer brought home with him a handful of clover from each corner of his neighbor's field his cattle would thrive during that year. A dream of a clover field meant health and prosperity. Occasionally a clover leaf is found that has four or more parts, and this is popularly accepted as a token of great good fortune.

In some English folk-lore it is said that the maids also search for the two-leaved clover, and sing:

> "A clover, a clover of two,
> Put in your right shoe,
> The first young man you meet,
> In field, street, or lane,
> You'll have him or one of his name."

In Scotland it was once thought that one who had a four-leaved clover on his person would immediately realize it if any one attempted to practice witchcraft upon him. Its virtue as a protection is referred to in these lines:

> "With a four-leaved clover, double-topped ash, and green-topped seave,
> You may go before the queen's daughter without asking leave."

This was accomplished by the combination. Seaves were the rushes from which the old rush lights were made. A reference to a different combination is also found in verse:

> "An even-leaved ash,
> And a four-leaved clover,
> You'll see your true love,
> 'Fore the day is over."

FLOWER LORE AND LEGEND

A four-leaved clover has long been supposed to invest the finder with great magical powers. Samuel Lover, in his Four-leaved Shamrock, gives voice to the superstition:

> "I'll seek a four-leaved shamrock, in all the fairy dells,
> And if I find the charmed leaves, oh, how I'll weave my spells.
> But I would play the enchanter's part in casting bliss around.
> Oh! not a tear or aching heart should in the world be found."

The fairy folk, in olden times when there were fairies, appropriated the clover as one of their especial plants. Whenever a fairy foot touched the ground there came up a four-leaved clover, possessed of magical power. Whoever found one was immediately taken under the protection of the little people. If a maiden, she saw her true love before the day closed. If a youth, his success in his wooing was assured. If a lover went on a journey and his sweetheart put a four-leaved clover in his shoe, he had a safe return. The fortunate possessors of this talisman were the only mortals who could hold converse with the fairies when they wished. As it brought all sorts of good luck at play, it is said to have caused the club, which in France is called 'Trefle,' to have been placed on the playing cards.

The clover grows in almost every part of the world and its uses are manifold. It enriches the ground where it grows. It provides fine pasturage and superior fodder. In times of famine in Ireland, it has been reported that when reduced to the last extremity, it was used as food by the starving people. It delights the senses with its beauty and sweet odor. The bee and the clover are fast friends, indeed one can 'scarcely exist without the other. Some years ago an effort was made to introduce the red clover

FLOWER LORE AND LEGEND

into Australia. It grew well, but failed to produce any seed. After one or two unsuccessful efforts, a number of bumblebees were imported from America and let loose when the clover had begun to blossom. From that time the red clover has been a success in Australia. Beekeepers claim that the finest quality of honey is obtained from the white clover. Perhaps this luxuriance of sweets, both of odor and taste, gave rise to the expression 'living in clover.' The earliest record of this saying appeared in 1710; and during that century it was frequently used to denote the height of luxurious living. In Flint, Michigan, a clover blossom a year is the rent charged the school board for a ninety-nine year lease of a school site. The use of the land for other than school purposes will terminate the lease. It has been decided to make a ceremonial feature of the payment of the rent each year. A member of the board is to be elected every spring to pluck a clover blossom from the lots and bear it to the owner or one of his heirs. The idea, however, is not new. The red clover has been chosen by the pupils of the public schools as the Vermont state flower. The literature of New England is filled with tributes to its virtues. Thoreau, in his Summer, likens the 'blushing fields of clover' to the 'western sky at evening.' Emerson, in both his prose and poetry, lauds it. The old country poets have not overlooked it. Dryden, Shakespeare, Burns, and Tennyson sing its praises, but it remains for the bards of Ireland to adequately portray the beauty of their national flower.

> "And so I love clover- it seems like a part
> Of the sacredest sorrows and joys of my hart;
> And wharever it blossoms; oh, thare let me bow
> And thank the good God as I'm thankin' Him now;
> And I pray to Him still fer the stren'th when I die,
> To go out in the clover and tell it good-by,
> And lovin'ly nestle my face in its bloom
> While my soul slips away on a breth of purfume."
> James Whitcomb Riley, The Clover.

FLOWER LORE AND LEGEND

THE BACHELOR BUTTONS

CELIBACY - DELICACY

"Blue, thou art intensely blue,
Flower, whence came thy dazzling hue?"

Montgomery.

Chiron, the leader of the centaurs, lived in a cave near the summit of Mount Pelion in Thessaly. He was renowned among the gods for his wisdom, for his skill in music and medicine, and for the use of weapons. He instructed the Grecian youths in these arts, and nearly all of his pupils distinguished themselves in Grecian story. Hercules was one of them. When he returned from the second of his great labors, the slaying of the hydra with nine heads, Chiron, his instructor, was the first to welcome him. In handling his weapons, an arrow, poisoned by the blood of the monster, fell upon the centaur's foot, piercing it with an ugly wound. A plant, with a blue flower, immediately sprang up at their feet, and Hercules, whom Chiron had instructed in the healing art, bound the root upon the wound. In a short time it was healed and ever since the plant has been known as centauria. The Abbe Barthelemy, in his history of the travels, writes that when Anacharsis visited Thessaly he went to the cave of Chiron on Mount Pelion, where the centaur showed him a plant with a ragged blue flower and explained to him its wonderful healing qualities. An eye-wash was prepared from the leaves, which was almost magical in its results. The secret of the preparation was known only to one person, to whom Chiron himself had entrusted it and who was to transmit it.

Under the name of cornflower, it has its place in history. It is the national flower of Germany, and is associated with the

FLOWER LORE AND LEGEND

beautiful and unfortunate Louise of Prussia, the mother of William, first Emperor of Germany. In October, 1806, was fought the double battle of Jena and Auerstadt. Queen Louise was forced to make her escape from Berlin with her two sons, the elder of whom was about nine years old. On the way to Koenigsberg the carriage broke down and they were obliged to alight and wait by the roadside until the damage was repaired. Seeing her distress, the little boys tried to console her, and one of them, the crown prince, said: "You are crying, mother?" "Yes," she replied, "I am weeping for Prussia." Then controlling herself, she continued: "We must not content ourselves with weeping; we must act." Putting an arm about each little lad, she endeavored to divert them by calling their attention to the great number of beautiful blue cornflowers that were growing near by. "Go," she said, "gather some of those flowers and I will make wreaths for you, and crown you king." Forgetting their troubles, the little fellows ran off and soon their mother's lap was filled with blossoms. When the wreath was made she placed it on the head of her eldest son. The other boy, the little William, begged her to make him one. Complying, she said, as she placed it on his little head: "Crowns mean very little sometimes." The boy clinched his fist, and standing erect, said: "When I am a man I will punish this Napoleon for making you feel so badly." They reached Koenigsberg safely, and before the close of the century that little boy was crowned Emperor of united Germany, and the successor to the great Napoleon became his prisoner. He always loved the cornflower, because it reminded him of his mother. He chose it for the floral emblem of the Germans, who call it the Kaiserblume. Pliny, writing of its medical properties, says, in his natural history, that twenty different remedies were prepared from the centauria. He cites the healing of Chiron's foot as evidence of its efficacy and states that pieces of meat were welded together simply by being boiled with the root. Another mythological account of the flower is the story of the youth named Cyanus, who was devoted to Flora, the goddess of

FLOWER LORE AND LEGEND

flowers. Of all her gifts he loved the cornflower the best. He was so enamored of it that he would scarcely leave the fields when it was in bloom. Always his garments were of the same bright blue color as his favorite flower.

Most of his time he spent in weaving garlands of the blossoms. One morning he was found dead in a corn field. In his hands and all about him were the blue flowers he had gathered. Flora grieved for the beautiful youth, and as a reward for his devotion she transformed him into the flower he had loved so well. There is a tradition that Cyanus is the original of Little Boy Blue of the old English nursery rhyme. In Russian folk-lore there is a story of a handsome youth named Basil, who was betrothed to a maiden of his own country. An enchantress named Russalka, who fell in love with him, failing to win him from his allegiance, enticed him into a field and changed him into the blue flower which in Russia is called basilek. Why the name bachelor button was given no one has ever been able definitely to decide. One old botanist of the sixteenth century writes that it received its name because of its resemblance to the "Jagged cloathe buttons anciently worne in this Kingdome." However that may be, there is no botanical authority for the name. In England there are twenty-one plants that have at some time or other been known as bachelor buttons. The plant is also known in England as bluet, blue bottle, blue bonnet, and logger-head. Queer, old names are break-your-spectacles and hawdods. Sometimes it was called hurt-cycle because the stems are very tough and turned the edges of the reapers' sickles in the days when reaping was done by hand.

The name logger-head was given on account of its resemblance to an old weapon of ancient times that consisted of a disk of iron with a long handle projecting from the center. A conflict with these weapons gave rise to the expression 'coming to logger-heads.'

FLOWER LORE AND LEGEND

There was a tradition among the country folk that the flower exerted a magical influence over the fortunes of lovers, and it was consequently the custom among the young men to carry it in their pockets. The blossom was to be picked with the morning dew still on it, and if, after twenty four hours the color was still bright and fresh, the wearer could be assured that he would be successful in his wooing. The expression, 'true blue,' had its origin in this superstition. It was also used as a love philter.

Sometimes maidens tested the faithfulness of their lovers by saying rhymes as they pulled the petals from the flowers, just as they do with the daisies. Miss Landon, in the Decision of the Flower, refers to this fortune-telling practice:

> "Now, gentle flower, I pray thee tell
> If my lover loves me and loves me well;
> So may the fall of the morning dew
> Keep the sun from fading thy tender blue,
> Now I number the leaves for my lot,
> He loves not. He loves me. He loves me not.
> He loves me. Yes ! thou last leaf, yes!
> I'll pluck thee not for the last sweet guess."

Mr. Coles, in Finger Ring-Lore, says that in divination the maids were careful to observe which way the flower leaned, and in connection quotes the following lines:

> "If on a shrub she casts her eye,
> That spoke her true love's secret sigh,
> Or else, alas, too plainly told,
> Her true love's faithless heart was cold."

The phrase, 'to wear bachelor buttons,' signifies being unmarried.

FLOWER LORE AND LEGEND

The flower has not attracted as much attention in literature as it deserves. Kryloff, a Russian poet, whose fables are household words in Russia, has made the basilek the subject of one of the most beautiful of his poetic tales. Although not definitely designated by Shakespeare, it is presumed to be the plant referred to in the Merry Wives of Windsor, when Fenton is playfully accused by his hostess of 'carrying his buttons' to determine the result of his love affairs. Chaucer, in the Romaunt of the Rose, writes of 'the fresh button so bright of hue.' Some writers contend that the blue cornflower was the blossom that Goethe chose as the floral oracle from which Marguerite was to learn the truth regarding Faust.

> "There is a flower, a deep blue flower.
> Sown by the wind, nursed by the shower,
> Over which love breathed a powerful spell,
> The truth of whispering hope to tell."

Miss Landon.

FLOWER LORE AND LEGEND

THE ROSE

LOVE

"If Zeus had willed it so,
That o'er the flowers one flower should reign a queen,
I know, ah, well I know,
The rose, the rose, that royal flower had been."

Sappho.

From the time of Midas, the King of Phrygia, whose rose gardens were the wonder of the ancient world, until the present time, the rose has reigned the queen of flowers. It was dedicated to Venus and was the emblem of joy and beauty. Comus, the god of feasting, was represented crowned with a garland of roses.

Almost every oriental nation had a legend of its origin. The Grecian poet, Anacreon, says that Venus, having been born from the sea, and Athena from the brain of Zeus, Gaea, the earth, was called upon for her contribution to Mount Olympus and modestly offered a green branch bearing a tiny bud. When some of the deities smiled at the insignificant offering, Jupiter commanded that the bud be sprinkled with nectar. Thereupon it slowly opened before the feasting gods and goddesses and became a full-blown white rose in all its regal splendor.

Its delicious perfume is accounted for by the story that Cupid, at the same feast, overturned a bowl of nectar, which, falling on the open flower, imparted to it the fragrance it still retains. Thus old Anacreon rhymed the tale:

"O, whence could such a plant have sprung,
Attend, for thus the tale is sung;

FLOWER LORE AND LEGEND

> Then, then in strange eventful hour
> The earth produced an infant flower;
> The gods beheld this brilliant birth,
> And hailed the rose, the boon of earth;
> And long the muses, heavenly maids,
> Have rear'd it in their tuneful shades."

Another story is that Venus, hurrying to Adonis with some of the same nectar, after he had been hurt by the wild boar, in alighting from her chariot stepped on a thorn. Where her blood stained the bush and the nectar was spilled there came forth the beautiful red rose. A favorite legend of the Greeks was that of Rodanthe, the beautiful and wise Queen of Corinth, who had so many suitors that she took refuge in the temple of Diana to escape from their importunity.

When three of the most persistent of her admirers attempted to follow her across the sacred threshold, she looked so beautiful in her excitement and indignation that the populace cried out, 'Let us make Rodanthe a goddess.' As she concealed herself in the inner shrine of Diana, Phoebus, the sun, Diana's brother, became so angered at the insult to his sister that he turned his burning gaze full upon the intruder. Rodanthe endeavored to leave the pedestal to escape his scorching rays, but her feet were held fast and her body and limbs turned into branches covered with leaves. In place of the Queen of Corinth there stood a rose tree, full of beautiful yellow flowers.

> "Tho' changed into a flower, her pomp remains,
> And lovely still, and still a queen she reigns."

The throng who were about the temple were turned into thorns to guard her beauty, and the too ardent lovers were transformed into a worm, a drone, and a butterfly. There is a Romanian tradition of a fair princess, who went to the sea to

FLOWER LORE AND LEGEND

bathe. The sun was so dazzled by her beauty that he stood still for three days. Of course, that interrupted the progress of night, and so upset things generally that Jupiter changed the princess into a rose tree. Whether this was before, after, or in the time of Joshua does not appear. In the garden was a lily and each aspired to be queen there. The rose supported her title by the poets. The height and dignity of the lily gave her an imperial appearance. Their respective rights were so warmly debated that Flora, the goddess, finally interfered as arbitrator. Cowper gives her decision in these words:

> "Yours," she said, "the noblest hue,
> And yours the statelier mien;
> And till a third surpasses you,
> Let each be deem'd a queen."

Sir John Maundeville, in his wonderful travels, tells of a maiden of Bethlehem who was accused of a crime and condemned to be burned. As the flames were kindled she prayed to the Lord that, as she was not guilty, He would cause her innocence to be known to all men. When the fires reached her they were immediately quenched, and the fagots that were burning became red rose trees, and those that were not kindled changed to white rose trees, both full of blossoms. These were the first tree roses ever seen on earth. The Romans were lavish in their use of roses. Whole shiploads were brought to Rome and there were shops in which nothing else was sold. At public games wreaths of them were given as prizes, and at private entertainments they were used in profusion for decorations. Nero, at some of his banquets, caused showers of rose leaves to be rained on his guests and had fountains of rose water playing in the hall. Cleopatra is said to have spent a fabulous sum to provide them for a feast which she gave for Marc Antony.

The proverbial bed of roses is not altogether a poetic

fiction. The Sybarites used to sleep on mattresses stuffed with roses, while Verres, a Roman politician, was accustomed to travel on a litter, the mattress of which was made of rose leaves. When he complained once of not sleeping well, Cicero sneeringly said that probably one of the rose leaves in his bed had become crumpled. Besides representing joy and beauty, the rose was also the emblem of silence. This idea is said to have originated when Cupid once gave a rose to Hippocrates, the god of silence, to bribe him not to reveal the indiscretions of Venus. The Romans, frequently, had a rose sculptured or painted on the ceilings of the banqueting hall to remind the guests that what was said at a festal gathering, under convivial conditions, was not to be repeated, but kept sub rosa, meaning under the rose.

There is also an historical account of the origin of this expression. From old inscriptions at Ravenna and Milan it is known that the Romans often directed, by will, that roses be strewn and planted upon their graves. This custom is alluded to by Anacreon and Propertius. Others regard them as emblems of an anxious clouded life, abounding in thorns and crosses. But though their beauties fade, the flowers come back with the return of spring. In Wales white rose trees are planted upon the graves of maidens and red bushes on those of persons who were distinguished for benevolence. The Scottish ballad of Fair Margaret and Sweet William tells of their lives, troubles, death, and burial, side by side:

> "Out of her breast there sprang a rose,
> And out of his a briar.
> They grew till they grew unto the church's top,
> And there they tied in a true love's knot,."

A tablet was erected in a church in England by Edward Rose, who died and was buried there. He left twenty pounds to the parish by his will upon condition that the rose trees in the cemetery should be kept up, and they are still cared for. It is thought that the following Christmas carol, which was popular in the fifteenth century, told the story of the conversion of France to Christianity:

> "The rose is the fairest flower of all,
> That evermore was, or evermore shall,
> The rose of ryse,
> Of all the flowers the rose bears prize.
> The rose it is the fairest flower,
> The rose is sweetest of odor,
> The rose in care is comforter,
> The rose in sickness it is salver,
> The rose so bright.
> In medicine it is most of might
> Witness these clerks that be wise.
> The rose is the flower most holden in prize.
> Therefore, me thinks, the fleur-de-lys
> Should worship the rose of ryse
> And be his thrall.
> And so should other flowers all.
> Many a knight with spear and lance,
> Followed that rose to his pleasance.
> When the rose betided a chance
> There followed all the flowers of France,
> In pleasance of the rose of true."

The words 'of ryse' as there used mean 'on the branch,' and the word 'salver' means 'Our Savior.'

There is an old tale which says that roses were sent by St. Dorothea from Paradise to St. Theophilus to keep a promise, made in life, that she would send back some word after death. In Persia the song of the nightingale is believed to be inspired by the odor of the rose. His followers say that the sweat of

FLOWER LORE AND LEGEND

Mohammed when on his way to heaven produced white roses, while that which dropped from Al Borak colored the yellow ones.

The custom of planting flowers in churchyards seems to have come from the belief that Paradise abounds with fragrant blossoms. The legend of Sir Owain refers to this. Anacreon, singing of the rose, says:

> "When pain afflicts and sickness grieves,
> Its juice the drooping heart relieves;
> And after death its odors shed
> A pleasing fragrance o'er the dead.
> And when its withering charms decay
> And sinking, fading die away,
> Triumphant, o'er the rage of time,
> It keeps the fragrance of its prime."

Virgil phrases the grief of Anchises thus:

> "Full canisters of fragrant lilies bring,
> Mixed with the purple roses of the spring,
> Let me with funeral flowers his body strew."

Manning says that the practice of planting rose bushes on graves in Ockley probably came from the Romans, as the old Roman road passes through the village, and it was anciently headquarters; and Evelyn, too, refers to the custom. It is said that roses fade on St. Magdalene's day. The rose played a very important part in medicine in the past. The oil, conserves, preparations from the plant leaves and from petals were used for nerve troubles, headaches, and indigestion. Thirty-two remedies are said to have been thus derived. The lotion was regarded as a certain cure for eruptions of the skin. The ointment was equally efficacious. Milto, a very beautiful maiden, used to take to the temple of Venus, every morning, a garland of fresh roses. It was all she had, as she was poor. When a tumor grew upon her face, entirely destroying her beauty, Venus appeared to her one night and told her to anoint her face with some of the leaves of the roses she had laid upon the altar. She did so, the tumor disappeared, and she was more beautiful than ever. She so attracted the attention of Cyrus, the younger, that she became his wife. In those luxurious times many of the nobles had baths filled with rose water. The young Romans were in the habit of sending baskets of roses to the ladies that they admired. Mia-rosa was a term of endearment used by the Roman lover to his betrothed.

The Persians regarded it as sacred, and associated it with the nightingale. It was believed by them that it burst into bloom at the song of the night-warbler. One day all the birds came before King Solomon, who understood their language, to complain of the nightingale, whom they charged with disturbing their slumbers by singing his mournful song all night long. The nightingale, being sent for, explained to the King that the rose waited for his call to come forth from the bud, and that his love for her was so great that he could not resist the temptation of seeing the beautiful flower unfold. The wise King acquitted him, and ever since the song of the nightingale is permitted to be heard in the stillness of the summer night. A carnival called the feast of roses was held in Persia during the entire time that the flower was in bloom.

The rose holds an important part in ecclesiastical history. It is especially dedicated to the Blessed Virgin, the Queen of Heaven, and is often introduced in some form in old paintings of the Madonna. A sacred legend states that the tomb of the Virgin was found filled with lilies and roses, after her assumption. The Golden Rose is a sacred ornament, which the Pope is accustomed to bless every year, on Lsetare Sunday, being the

FLOWER LORE AND LEGEND

fourth Sunday in Lent. It is always of exquisite workmanship, and is sometimes set with jewels. It symbolizes the beauty and majesty of Christ. The day of the ceremony is called Rose Sunday, and rose colored vestments and draperies are substituted for the purple ones in use during Lent. The blessing of the Golden Rose takes place in the hall of vestments and the mass in the papal chapel.

After the ceremony it is sometimes conferred upon some noted church, upon a state or municipal government, or upon some distinguished individual, who has rendered great service to the church. The last one was bestowed by Leo XIII upon Marie Henriette, Queen of Belgium, in 1893. The same one is used each year until it has been disposed of. The flower is emblematic of the frailty of human life, and the indestructible metal signifies the immortality of the soul. There was once a Princess of Hungary, who was both beautiful and good. From her childhood she had devoted her life to deeds of charity. When she was fifteen she was married to Prince Ludwig of Thuringia, who sympathized with her in her benevolent plans, but his mother and sister opposed them, and in the Prince's absence were very unkind to the Princess Elizabeth. There was a famine in Thuringia and her wisdom saved the lives of many of the subjects. She directed that the food that was in store should be divided into portions, so that the supply should last until the harvest, and she herself shared in it the same as the people. Much of her time was spent in visiting the sick. One day when she was leaving the castle with a supply of food she met her husband returning from the hunt.

He demanded to know what she had under her cloak, and when she hesitated, fearing his displeasure because she deprived herself of the necessities of life, he drew the cloak aside, and found that her basket was full of beautiful white roses. Doubtless her surprise was as great as his. St. Elizabeth of Hungary is

FLOWER LORE AND LEGEND

represented in one of the eleven pictures painted by Murillo for the charity hospital in Seville.

The poet, Dante, recognizes the rose as the symbol of the Blessed Virgin: "The rose wherein the Word divine was made incarnate." He employs it also to describe the whole army of saints: "Advancing like a rose unfolding its petals." The holy multitude in heaven he likens: "In fashion to snow-white roses." As an emblem of the frailty of life, it has also been embodied in verse:

> "Each morn a thousand roses brings, you say;
> Yes, but where leaves the rose of yesterday?"

Thus sings the 'Rubdiydt of Omar Khayyam. And William Cullen Bryant wrote:

> "The rose that lives its little hour,
> Is prized beyond the sculptured flower."

It is the national emblem of England, and figures conspicuously in the history of that country. In the days of the Roman occupation, England was known as Albion, probably because of its wide expanse of white chalk cliffs. The Latin word alba means white. The romancing Pliny suggests that it was so called because of the great number of white roses which grew there. However this may be, the rose was not recognized as the royal flower until some centuries later. King Edward I, whose reign ended in 1307, assumed it as his personal badge, but it made its first appearance upon the great seal of the kingdom during the reign of Edward IV. This monarch also caused to be issued a gold coin bearing a rose upon both faces, which was known as the rose-noble. In the fifteenth century the Wars of the Roses forever associated the flower with English history. Shakespeare, no doubt, followed some old tradition in the account he gave in his Henry VI. He narrates a quarrel in the old temple garden between the Duke of York and the Earl of Somerset. Finding that their followers are becoming excited, the Duke suggests that they 'shall in dumb significance proclaim their thoughts,' adding:

> "Let him who is a true-born gentleman,
> And stands upon the honor of his birth,
> If he supposes I have pleaded truth,
> From off this briar pluck a white rose with me."

To which the Earl replies:

> "Let him who is no coward nor no flatterer,
> But dares maintain the party of the truth,
> Pluck a red rose flower from this briar with me."

The respective knights gathered the different-hued roses and Warwick foretells the terrible strife that "shall send between the white rose and the red, thousands of souls to death, and deadly night."

The wars lasted thirty years, and then a Princess of York married a Prince of Lancaster, and the roses were united. An English writer claims that the expression sub rosa had its origin at this time. Two taverns, one at the side and one opposite the houses of parliament, displayed as signs the red and white roses, respectively, and each was frequented by the adherents of their emblem. As private conferences were held and measures requiring secrecy were discussed, in referring to their transactions, they were said to have taken place 'under the rose.' There is a portrait of Queen Elizabeth with a rose in her ear, which illustrates this expression. When so worn it means, 'Hear all and say nothing.'

FLOWER LORE AND LEGEND

In France it has also played a part in politics and history. A singular custom, the origin of which is not known, existed and was observed until the seventeenth century. All the French nobles, even those of royal blood, were required on a certain day to present roses to the parliament at Paris. The presentation was made by one of the peers and it was regarded as a great honor to be selected for this office. On the day of the presentation a splendid breakfast was served and every member of parliament was presented with a garland and a huge bouquet of roses.

Another French festival, which has only recently been discontinued, was the Fete d'la Rosiere, which took place at Salency, near Paris. It was instituted in 480 by the Bishop of Noyon, and consisted of publicly crowning with roses the most amiable, modest, and virtuous maiden in the village, who was selected by the vote of the villagers. To provide for the expenses of the feast the bishop set apart a portion of his own domain, which was known as the manor of the rose. The first young girl selected as the Rose of Salency was the bishop's sister.

In the day of chivalry those taking part in tournaments often wore a rose as an evidence of their devotion to love and beauty. Among the knights there was an 'Order of the Rose,' the insignia of which was a rose embroidered on the sleeve as a sign that gentleness accompanied courage, and that beauty was the reward of valor. In the fifteenth and sixteenth centuries, there are on record several instances where roses have been used in payment of rent. In 1758, the Bishop of Ely granted to Sir Christopher Hatton certain valuable property for a term of twenty-one years, in consideration of payment of 'one red rose' annually on Midsummer Day, but reserving to himself the privilege of gathering twenty bushels of roses yearly.

In the quaint, little town of Manheim, in Pennsylvania, on the second Sunday in June each year, a unique celebration

FLOWER LORE AND LEGEND

occurs, in the payment to the oldest lineal descendant of Baron Stiegel one red rose, the annual rent for land given by him a century and a half ago to the Zion Lutheran Church. This curious requirement is set forth in a deed in due and legal form, providing that 'unto the said Henry William Stiegel, his heirs, and assigns, at the said town of Manheim, in the month of June, yearly, one red rose shall be paid, if the same shall be lawfully demanded.' Twice this rent was paid to the Baron himself. Then, for one hundred and twenty years, the strange obligation was lost sight of, and became a tradition, remembered only by a .few of the oldest inhabitants.

About 1890, an antiquarian delving into the history of the town discovered the old deed. A large, handsome church now occupies the ground donated by the Baron. There had been no violation of the terms of the deed, as during that time the rose had not been demanded. In 1892 the church authorities determined to revive the payment and make it an interesting ceremony. They had no knowledge of the descendants of Baron Stiegel, but preparations for the festival were made and duly chronicled in the daily papers, with the result that one of the heirs who lived in Virginia came forward. Since then others have been heard from and each year there is a goodly representation of the Baron's family at Manheim's 'Feast of Roses.'

The old-fashioned gardens of our great grandmothers were full of rose bushes, which gave pleasure to every sense, even that of taste, for the cookbooks of the seventeenth and eighteenth centuries contained many recipes in which the rose in some form or other played a part. Here is one copied from an old manuscript cook-book, compiled by a great-great-grandmother, when she was eighteen, probably in anticipation of her marriage:

"To make Conserve of Roses- Take one quart of rose water, one quart of rain water, filtered; boil in the water a pound

FLOWER LORE AND LEGEND

of red rose leaves. When the leaves are boiled to pulp, add three pounds of loaf sugar. Add it one pound at a time and let it boil five minutes between each pound, then put it in pots."

The same generation kept a rose jar on the mantel in the best room, filled with rose leaves, and when the lid was removed on state occasions the quaint pungent odor filled the room. More than a century ago there was in Paris an association of literary men who called themselves 'The Society of the Rose,' and their place of meeting was known as the 'Thicket of Roses.'

In order to become a member it was necessary not only to be a congenial spirit, but also to have written a song of the rose that had been passed upon and accepted by the other members. Thus, from the day of Isaiah, its praises have been sung by the great writers of every age. Chaucer, in The Romaunt of the Rose, tells many of the medieval legends. Spenser, Southey, and Byron all sing of it. But Moore is pre-eminent in his devotion to it, his poems abounding with beautiful allusions. As long as roses bloom his memory will keep green.

> "Long, long be my heart with such memories filled,
> Like the vase in which roses have once been distilled.
> You may break, you may shatter the vase if you will,
> But the scent of the roses will hang round it still."

Thomas Moore, The Farewell.

FLOWER LORE AND LEGEND

THE LILY

PURITY - MAJESTY

"Consider the lilies of the field, how they grow; they toil not, neither do they spin. And yet, I say unto you, that even Solomon in all his glory was not arrayed like one of these-" Matthew vi, 28-29.

> "Yet the great ocean hath no tone or power,
> Mightier to reach the soul in thought's hushed hour,
> Than yours, ye lilies, chosen thus and graced."

Mrs. Hemans.

From the earliest period of Christianity Easter has been regarded by the church as the queen of festivals. The fixing of the date of its observance is a complicated and difficult process. Originally it fell upon the same day as the Jewish Passover, but very early in ecclesiastical history serious controversies arose as to the exact day upon which the festival should be celebrated. These differences were settled by the Council of Nicea, in A.D. 325, which decreed that the first Sunday after the full moon, following the vernal equinox, March 21st, should be observed as Easter day. The name Easter is supposed to be derived from Eastra or Ostera, who, in Teutonic mythology, was the goddess of spring and the personification of the dawn. Her feast was held by the Anglo-Saxons in the spring time. The early missionaries, finding it impossible to do away with its observance, endeavored, as they did in many instances, to give the festival a Christian significance, utilizing the awakening of spring and the release of water from the icy bonds of winter as symbolizing the resurrection and the power of Christ over death and the grave.

FLOWER LORE AND LEGEND

Easter is pre-eminently the festival of flowers. Not only are the churches and homes decorated with cut flowers, and blossoming plants, but these beautiful messengers are used to convey the glad Easter greeting from friend to friend. While all flowers are appropriate, the white lily, symbol of purity, majesty, and innocence, has come to be the generally accepted favorite. The lily family includes flowers of many forms and colors. The name is often incorrectly applied to plants of distinctly different species, as the iris, the lotus, and the pond lily. All through history and literature the rose and the lily have gone hand in hand. Although among the Greeks and Romans the rose was the favorite, the lily was held in high esteem, and in Egypt, India, and Arabia it was pre-eminent. Its appearance with the lotus was of very ancient date. Among the ancients it was known as the flower of Juno, and was consecrated to that imperious goddess as the rose was dedicated to Venus.

One legend as to its origin is that when Hercules was born, his father, Jupiter, was desirous that he should rank with the other deities. In order that this might be, the child must be endowed with immortality. Jupiter, therefore, ordered Somnus, the god of slumber, to prepare a sleeping draught, disguised in nectar, which he persuaded Juno to drink. The Queen immediately fell into a deep sleep, and while she slept Jupiter placed the infant at her breast that he might absorb the celestial nourishment which would insure immortality. The babe was hungry and drew the lacteal fluid faster than he could swallow it. Some drops falling to the earth, there sprang up the white flower, which was ever after to rival the rose. Another version is that, up to that time, the lily had been of a bright orange color, and that every blossom that was touched by a drop of the precious liquid immediately turned to a pure white. Still another tradition tells that the white lily was so much admired by all who saw it that Venus, who hated Juno, was very jealous, and one day inserted a colored pistil to mar the pure whiteness of the blossom. The flower blushed with shame at a deed so unworthy of a goddess, and the origin of the red and the tiger lily is thus accounted for. There has been much discussion as to the particular lily referred to by the Savior in the Sermon on the Mount. Some contend that it was the white lily to which Solomon in his glory was not to be compared. But the lily of Palestine is by most authorities conceded to be of a bright orange red, corresponding to the red prairie lily. This variety abounds in the neighborhood of Galilee, and in season the fields present a gorgeous appearance.

There is a tradition that prior to the crucifixion all the lilies in Palestine were white. But when Christ walked in Gethsemane the night before His death every flower of the garden bowed its head before His agony except the lily, who said: "He chose me as the most beautiful of all, and gorgeous above the greatest of kings. I will stand erect and comfort Him with my beauty and fragrance." As the Savior passed He stopped for a moment to gaze at the beautiful flower shining in the moonlight. The lily was so overcome by His humility and her own unworthiness that she blushed a deep red and bowed her head in shame. From that time it became the red lily and has never held its head erect. There is no flower that has so many religious associations. It is the emblem of purity and truth. The Italian painters have made frequent use of this in symbolism. The Angel of the Annunciation is represented bearing in his hand white lilies. In many pictures of the Virgin Mother they appear in some form.

In 1048 Garcia, the fourth King of Navarre, was dangerously ill, and he dreamed that he saw the Virgin emerging from one of the white lilies in the gardens of the palace. The sight induced a calm sleep from which he awoke much refreshed. On his recovery he instituted the order of the Blessed Lady of the Lily. Its members were the King and thirty-eight

FLOWER LORE AND LEGEND

knights, each of whom wore upon his breast a silver lily, and was pledged to deeds of charity and purity of life. An order of the lily was also established in 1408 by Ferdinand of Aragon. The members were sworn into the service of Our Blessed Lady. But although the lily seems to be especially associated with the Madonna, legend also connects it with St. Catherine of Alexandria. Her father was Costis, the Emperor. Proud of his daughter's extraordinary abilities, he superintended her studies with much care. To her great sorrow he refused to accept the truths of Christianity, and although by her arguments drawn from the philosophers and the gospels she had convinced all of her masters, with her father they proved of no avail. After she had spent much time in fasting and prayer for his conversion, one night the Emperor had a dream. He was walking with his daughter, who talked to him on the subject that was nearest her heart. They came to a place where two paths met, one smooth and shaded, leading to a green valley; the other narrow, steep, and stony. Catherine turned into the narrow path, and, looking back at him with longing in her eyes, disappeared. Costis was hesitating which way to take, when a delicate perfume attracted him. It seemed to float down the narrow path and to draw him irresistibly in that direction.

    As he followed his daughter and drew near the top of the hill the perfume grew stronger, and when he reached the summit he found himself in a field of white lilies, extending up to a golden gate, which dazzled his eyes with its glory. Falling down on his knees among the flowers Costis vowed to renounce his false gods and to adopt Christianity. As he was kneeling his daughter reappeared and admitted him through the golden gateway. When he awoke from his dream the Emperor sent for the Princess and rejoiced her heart by accepting the Christian faith. The lily, which up to this time had been without perfume, now became the sweetest of flowers. By common consent it was dedicated to St. Catherine. But the lily, as well as the rose,

FLOWER LORE AND LEGEND

yielded to the beauty of the mystical Flower of Jesse, Our Savior, of the root of Jesse. In an ancient carol, known to have been sung about 1426, appear these verses:

> "Of lily, of rose of ryse,
> Of primrose, and of fleur-de-lys,
> Of all the flowers at my device,
> That Flower of Jesse yet bears the price,
> As most of heal
> To slake our sorrows every deal.
> I pray the flowers of this countree,
> Wherever ye go, wherever ye be,
> Hold up the Flower of good Jesse,
> For your freshness and your beauty,
> As fairest of all,
> And ever was and ever shall."

Another tale explains why St. Joseph is so often represented holding a lily in his hand. Among the Hebrews, although the young men and maidens associated together, when a girl was of marriageable age her father or mother and sometimes the High Priest selected a husband for her. When the time came to choose a husband for the Virgin Mary, who was an attendant at the temple, there were many who aspired to the honor. The High Priest prayed for a sign that he might choose aright. As was the custom in those days, the young men all carried staffs. One day they were told to leave them in the sanctuary of the temple until the next morning. At the appointed time, it was found that Joseph's staff was covered with beautiful white lilies, which had sprouted from it during the night. The plant, according to ancient testimony, was prolific in medicinal properties, no less than twenty one remedies being derived from it. As an antidote for serpent bites, or for poison by fungi, it was regarded as almost infallible. For a hair restorative the roots were boiled in olive oil. Among the Hebrews the lily was a cherished flower. It is referred

FLOWER LORE AND LEGEND

to frequently in the Old Testament. In the decoration of the magnificent temple of Solomon the tops of the pillars in the porches were ornamented with lilies, and they were also wrought in the crown of King Solomon.

When Judith undertook to deliver her people from the Assyrians and left Bethulia to go to the tent of Holofernes, the captain of the besieging army, she wore them as a wreath. These numerous references have caused it to receive particular notice in Jewish commentaries. A learned writer of the eleventh century, in giving a beautiful interpretation, says that it is one of the few flowers described in ancient Hebrew literature. "A white flower of sweet but narcotic perfume. It has six petals and six stamens, and one pistil, representing the thirteen attributes of God. The heart of the blossom is always turned upward, and it is often found growing among thorns, symbolizing the trust in Jehovah which His children should feel even amid afflictions. The Semitic name of the lily is Azucena, which is translated Susannah. In Spain the flower is still known by that name."

Its beauty is not its only claim to consideration. The roots and stalks of the plant have always been valued as food in Eastern countries. While no flower garden in Japan is complete without it as an ornament, there is never a well-chosen menu which does not include the products of the plant in some form. An analysis of the bulbs made by the Japanese government some years ago demonstrated that they contained over ninety-eight per cent, of nutritious matter. Their cultivation is an important industry. They are usually boiled and eaten with sugar, or cooked with rice. Americans use them for salad. A fine, starchy flour, useful in pastry and fine cooking, is made from them. The Aniu, an aboriginal race, supposed at one time to have inhabited the whole of Japan, but now like the American Indian, reduced to a few scattered groups, still depend chiefly for their vegetable diet upon certain species. There has been some investigation by the

FLOWER LORE AND LEGEND

United States in regard to the cultivation of the lily for culinary purposes, but no report has yet been issued.

The beautiful white lily, with which the churches at Easter are decorated, originated in Japan, and was carried to the Bermudas by some flower-loving sea captain between two and three hundred years ago. Owing to the advantages of climate it has developed a beauty and hardiness which has made it the admiration of two continents. In 1875 there was brought from Bermuda to Philadelphia two plants in blossom which were given to a local florist. In about three years they had increased to one hundred, and had attracted the attention of other dealers. As the bulbs raised in this country do not produce as fine blossoms as those developed in Bermuda, the number imported every year is enormous, and the cultivation has become one of the leading industries of the islands. In 1903 a bulletin was issued by the United States which said that three million bulbs were imported annually from Bermuda.

The Song of Solomon exalts the lily above all other flowers. Dante represented the glorious multitude, with Beatrice in their midst, as scattering lilies around them. It is only when he is cleansed from all sin that he deems himself worthy to even look upon the pure lily that blooms in Paradise. Leigh Hunt, in the Song of the Lilies, says:

> "We are lilies fair,
> The flower of virgin light.
> Nature held us forth and said,
> Lo! my thoughts are white.
> Ever since then angels
> Hold us in their hands.
> You may see them when they take
> In pictures their sweet stands."

FLOWER LORE AND LEGEND

The Germans have a saying that if, when a lily is picked a certain prayer is said, the flower will protect against witchcraft. In Spain, if a person had been transformed into an animal by sorcery, it was believed that a lily would restore him. A bibliography of the lily would refer to almost every poet of note from Homer to Tennyson, and the grand woman of America, who has only recently passed into 'the beauty of the lilies,' has glorified them in her masterpiece:

> "In the beauty of the lilies, Christ was born across the sea,
> With the glory in His bosom that transfigures you and me;
> As He died to make men holy, let us die to make men free,
> While God is marching on."

Julia Ward Howe, The Battle Hymn of the Republic.

FLOWER LORE AND LEGEND

THE PASSION FLOWER

RELIGIOUS SUPERSTITION

"Many a sign
Of the great sacrifice which won us Heaven,
The woodman and the mountaineer can trace
On rock, on herb, and flower. And be it so!
They do not wisely that, with hurried hand,
Would pluck these salutary fancies forth
From the strong soil within the peasant's breast,
And scatter them- far, far too fast- away
As worthless weeds. Oh ! little do we know
When they have soothed, when saved."

Mrs. Hemans, Wood Walk.

Passiflora is the generic name for a large number of very interesting plants, mostly of the climbing order. Their great attractiveness lies in the unusualness of the blossom. The principal variety and the one which gave the name to the whole species is known to all the world as the passion flower. It is a native of South America and it is said that when the early missionaries, who so quickly followed in the steps of the Spanish invaders, first saw it hanging in festoons from the forest trees, with its luxuriant purple and white blossoms, they believed it to have been sent as an aid to them in the conversion of the natives to the Christian religion. The first account of the flower and its interpretation was written by Monardes, a physician and botanist of the sixteenth century. This description, with a drawing of the plant, was brought to Rome by an Augustinian friar, Emanuel de Villegas, a native of the City of Mexico. It attracted the attention of Jacomo Bosio, the historian of the Knights of Malta, who was at the time engaged upon his great work, The Cross

FLOWER LORE AND LEGEND

Triumphant. Bosio at first hesitated about introducing into his book the account of what he called so stupendous a flower. But the description of de Villegas, having been corroborated by other travelers from New Spain, he decided to mention it, as a most wonderful illustration of the cross triumphant in the world of nature. His description of the plant created a great excitement among the botanists and theologians of that day and led to its introduction soon after, into both Spain and Italy. Before 1625 some remarkable specimens had been produced in the gardens of the Cardinal Fornese, who was one of the most distinguished patrons of horticulture in Europe. Aldinus of Cesera, who was both the Cardinal's physician and the keeper of his garden, writes: "This wonderful plant is sung by poets, celebrated by orators, reasoned about by philosophers, praised by physicians for its numberless virtues, wondered at by theologians, and venerated by all Christians."

The symbolical interpretations of the flower by both Bosio and Aldinus are most interesting; but as Bosio had never seen it, it is probable that the one given by Aldinus more nearly corresponds to that which sentiment may really find in it. The column rising from the center of the flower represents the upright beam of the cross. Above this are three, and sometimes four, small stems which are the nails. Surmounting the column is the corona, which symbolizes the crown of thorns, and around it is a veil of fine hairs colored like peacock's feathers, seventy-two in number, which are said to correspond to the number of thorns of which the crown was composed. The filaments suggest the scourge by which the Savior was smitten. The small seed vessel is the sponge filled with vinegar, which was offered to quench His thirst. The five deep red spots upon each of the leaves are the five wounds. Hence the name given it by the Spaniards, flower of the five wounds. The resemblance of the blossom, when not entirely open, to a star, refers to the star seen by the three wise men. The five sepals and the five petals indicate the ten apostles,

FLOWER LORE AND LEGEND

Peter, who denied our Lord, and Judas, who betrayed Him, being omitted. The purple blossoms are the purple robe which was put on Christ in mockery. The white blossoms represent the purity and brightness of the Son of God. The flowers grow singly on the stem, typifying the loneliness of Christ. The leaves are set on the stock singly, for there is one God, but are triplicate in form to testify to the Trinity. The plant is a vine and requires support. So the Christian, who would aspire, needs Divine assistance. The bell shape assumed by the flower when opening and fading meant that God had not chosen to reveal the mysteries of His power until such time as should in His infinite wisdom seem best. If the plant is cut down, it grows again readily; therefore, whoever bears in his heart the love of God cannot be harmed by the evil of the world. Such was the symbolism attributed to the plant by the old Spanish missionaries. All Christendom seems to have accepted their ideas and they have become a part of the folk-lore of the Christian world.

The first passion flower exhibited in England was brought from Virginia by some of the colonial adventurers, and attracted almost as much attention there as its South American relative attracted, at the same time, in Italy and Spain; but, while the beauty and sweetness of the flower was extolled by English writers, the religious significance attributed to it was criticized. Parkinson, one of the botanists of the time, suggested naming it clematis virginiana, meaning the virgin climber, partly with reference to the province from which it came and also in honor of Queen Elizabeth, the glory of whose reign was still fresh in the minds of the people.

The flower, however, has still retained its Italian name and much of its religious association. For church decorations it is deemed a worthy companion of the rose and the lily. It is especially appropriate for memorial decorations. A wreath of

FLOWER LORE AND LEGEND

passion flowers was, by the express request of Queen Victoria, laid upon the last resting place of the martyred Abraham Lincoln. It is considered a suitable decoration for All Saints day. S. F. Smith wrote these appropriate lines:

> "They called the purple circlet, there,
> The crown of thorns 'twas His to wear,
> And every leaf seemed to their eye
> Memorial of his agony.
> 'Tis fancy all- yet do not scorn
> The thought of adoration born,
> But let each flower that meets our sight
> Recall the Lord of life and light."

The flower also has its place in modern religious art and architecture. Workers in stained glass and mural decoration have made use of it almost to the exclusion of some of the older floral symbols. It holds an especially noteworthy place in the ironwork of the beautiful choir screens in the Cathedrals at Lichfield and at Hereford. In Lockhart's story of Valerius, a young Christian maiden is referred to as gathering, in the garden of a stately Roman villa, a flower which symbolizes some of the deepest mysteries of her religion.

That the author had in mind the passion flower there can be no reasonable doubt, but it is difficult to reconcile Lockhart's well-known classical accuracy with the fact that this flower was not known in Europe until several hundred years later than the scene in which the story is laid. Many poets, like Rapin, have found the flower 'too suggestive a theme to pass unmoved' and numerous verses have been written of it. Treatises have been printed, explaining its botanical or religious significance. To the Christian world at large, whether in its native South American home, in the gardens of Europe, or in the more tropical parts of our own country, it speaks symbolically:

FLOWER LORE AND LEGEND

"Art thou a type of beauty, or of power,
Of sweet enjoyment, or disastrous sin?
For each thy name denoteth, passion flower!
Oh, no! thy pure corolla's depth within
We trace a holier symbol, yes, a sign
'Twixt God and man;
It is the Cross!

Sir Aubrey De Vere, The Passion Flower.

FLOWER LORE AND LEGEND

THE MANDRAKE

RARITY

"And shrieks like mandrakes, torn out of the earth,
That living mortals, hearing them, ran mad."

Shakespeare.

There are few plants around which has gathered such a wealth of legend and tradition as has accumulated around the flower known as the mandrake. From the earliest times to which history takes us it was held in veneration by the inhabitants of the Eastern lands. Many of the superstitions associated with it are unpleasant and most of them are uncanny. The plant itself is insignificant. The leaves rise directly from the ground. They are sharp-pointed, hairy, and of a vivid, dark-green color. The flower is a sickly white, veined with purple. The root is long and shaped like a parsnip. It is often forked, causing fanciful persons to imagine that it bears some resemblance to a rudely formed human figure. To this fanciful likeness is due many of the superstitions that cluster around the plant. It was supposed by the Romans to be under the especial protection of Atropos, the sablerobed, grim-visaged fate, who remorselessly severed the thread of life which was spun by Clotho and twisted by Lachesis. By the Greeks it was known as Circean and was dedicated to Circe, the daughter of the sun, the golden-haired enchantress, celebrated for her knowledge of witchcraft, who so nearly accomplished the undoing of those companions of Ulysses, when they accompanied him on his wanderings after the sacking of Troy back to Ithaca. The roots cling tenaciously to the earth, and it was a current superstition that whenever the plant was gathered it gave vent to terrible shrieks and groans that sounded almost human, and were said to cause instant death to any creature who heard them. As the plants held an important place as a medical remedy among the ancients, an ingenious, if rather inhuman, method of obtaining them was devised. The persons who gathered them, after carefully stopping their ears, fastened a dog securely to the plant by his tail. He was then driven or enticed away. Thus the root was dragged out of the earth, and the unfortunate animal dropped dead upon the spot as the plant emitted the most heart-rending screams.

An old Jewish writer is authority for this tradition, but it seems to have been widely current. Shakespeare makes several allusions to it. At a later period a belief seems to have prevailed that if gathered at holy times and with the repetition of certain invocations, which were probably anything but holy, the Evil One would aid the seeker of the plant, and it could be obtained with safety. Pliny writes that in Rome it was the custom of those who sought the roots to make three circles around the plant with the point of a sword, and then having turned toward the west they proceeded to dig it up. From ancient times, also, came the superstition that the plant grew only in dark places and thrived under the shadow of a gallows, near a gibbet, or where criminals were buried.

In later times the plant was looked upon as a preventative of illness and all danger. Mountebank doctors took advantage of the popular superstition and carved the roots into idols, which were regarded as oracles and treasured as safeguards against evil. The power was also attributed to them of increasing money, which was placed near them. These images were much valued in Germany. A letter written by a German burgomaster in Leipsic to his brother in Regi in 1675, which has been preserved, shows how the mandrake was regarded by the credulous at that time. He had heard that his brother had been visited by misfortune. He therefore paid sixty-four thalers for the little figure, which he sent to his brother, with these words:

FLOWER LORE AND LEGEND

"When thou hast the earthman in thy house, let it rest for three days without approaching it; then place it in warm water. Afterward with the water sprinkle all the animals and the sills of the house, and it shall go better with thee if thou shalt serve the earth manikin rightly."

An Italian writer says that some of the ladies of Italy have been known to pay twenty-five or thirty ducats in gold for one of these charms. They were introduced into England during the reign of King Henry VIII, where they found ready purchasers. Gararde, a celebrated botanist of the sixteenth century, endeavored to convince the credulous and superstitious that they were being duped, but he does not seem to have been very successful. As late as 1810 these images were seen exposed for sale in several of the seaport towns of France. If properly secured, it was supposed to become a familiar spirit, which spoke in oracles and brought good luck. In the fourteenth verse of Chapter 30 of Genesis, it is said: "And Reuben went, in the days of the wheat harvest, and found mandrakes in the field, and brought them unto his mother Leah."

The leaves of the plant emit a powerful odor, which, when fresh, was supposed to be a baneful poison. The remedy, according to Pliny, was to soak them in brine. Persons ignorant of this fact have been said to have been made dumb by inhaling the odor to excess. In spite of this, the plant was credited with many curative properties. The juice, mixed with rose oil, was used for diseases of the eye. Administered in suitable quantities it was a wonderful narcotic. It was also beneficial for the bites of serpents and for incisions or injuries to the body. It was used to produce insensibility to pain, and in soothing nervous disorders, and for love potions.

Among the numerous names by which it has been referred to are several that seem to indicate its association with

FLOWER LORE AND LEGEND

the powers of evil. Among the Arabs it was known as the devil's apple and the devil's food. Because of the luminous quality of the leaves at night it was sometimes called the devil's candle. Moore alludes to this fact in his Lallah Rookh:

> "Such rank and deadly luster dwells,
> As in those hellish fires that light
> The mandrake's charnel leaves at night."

It is also sometimes called the may or love apple. The fruit when ripe is like a golden globe. That these uncanny beliefs continued almost to modern times is shown in an anecdote for which Madam du Noyer is authority. On the murder of the Marechal de Fabert, which was popularly attributed to his having broken a contract with the devil, two mandrakes of extraordinary beauty were found in his rooms. These were considered by his friends as conclusive evidence of the compact of which they failed, however, to find any tangible proof.

In literature the mandrake has been the subject of much study and conjecture. A great deal has been written of its magical qualities. Shakespeare and Moore both make frequent references to it, but the simpler poets, in spite of its historical interest, seem not to find it an agreeable subject for their verses.

> "The blushing peach and glossy plum there lies,
> And with the mandrake tempt your hands and eyes."

Jane Turrell, In Tuckermans America.

FLOWER LORE AND LEGEND

THE MARIGOLD

CRUELTY IN LOVE

"Nor shall the marigold unmentioned die,
Which Acis once found out in Sicily;
She Phoebus loves, and from him draws his hue,
And ever keeps his golden beam in view."

Rapin.

"Coarse marigold, in days of yore,
I scorned thy tawny face,
But since my plants are frail and few,
I've given thee welcome place."

Mrs. Sigourney.

The marigold is a classic. It is supposed to have been the gold-flower of the ancient Greeks, and was used by them for decoration at their most important festivals. Rapin, the French poet, gives an account of the origin of the flower. Of all the gods who dwelt on Mount Olympus, Apollo was the most attractive, and all the foolish nymphs and shepherdesses vied with each other to gain his attention. Among the attendants of his sister, Diana, were four little wood-nymphs, who accompanied her when she went hunting. Every one of them fell in love with the beautiful sun-god. They were so jealous of each other that they quarreled continually. When Diana discovered this she was much displeased and changed them all into gold-flowers. Ever since that time yellow has been the color that represents jealousy. Chaucer probably had this in mind, when in the Knight's Tale, the Queen refers to "Jealousy- that wears of yellow goldes, a garland."

FLOWER LORE AND LEGEND

By the Romans the flower was known as calendula, or the flower of all months, because it was said to be in blossom during every month of the year. This may have been true of warm Eastern countries, but it is not of France, England, or America, where the flower is reckoned as one of the blossoms of the late summer and early autumn. However, it originated in Asia. The Swedish botanist, Linnaeus, who is regarded as the highest authority, has noted that the flower usually opens in the morning, after the sun is well up, and closes about three o'clock in the afternoon. In India the Buddhists hold it as sacred to the great goddess Maha-devi. Her trident emblem is adorned with these flowers, and both men and women wear garlands of them at her sacred festivals. In Provence the flower is known as gauchefer, meaning left-hand iron, probably because its round, brilliant disk suggests the polished shield once borne by warriors on the left arm. The common French name is souci du jardin. The old spelling was soulsi, which shows its derivation from sol, the sun. The full name was solsequieum, which means sun follower. By the Germans it is called gelt or gold-flower. It was introduced into England about 1573 and immediately became very popular. The botanical records of the period mentioned it as mary gowles. In some parts of England it is still spoken of as gowles or goulans. Another old name, which is not entirely obsolete, is ruddes. It was also often called simply golde! A writer of the time of Elizabeth says: "Maydens make garlands of it which they wear to feests and brydeales." To dream of marigolds was regarded as fortunate. It foretold a happy marriage, wealth, riches, and success.

From Breton comes a tale that, if a maiden touches a marigold with her bare foot, she will be able, afterwards, to understand the language of birds. In the early dawn of Christianity, when the minds of the people were still filled with the myths and mystical rites of pagan worship, it is not surprising that the early Christians should have transferred many of the old

FLOWER LORE AND LEGEND

poetic thoughts to the worship of God and His saints, nor that beautiful flowers should be associated with noble deeds, or held as memorials of heroic sacrifices. Thus it was not unusual to prefix the name of the Virgin Mary to anything that was regarded as especially beautiful. As the golde was one of the most admired of flowers, in time it became known as the mary-golde. In an old church calendar it is designated as the appropriate flower for the twenty-fifth of March, or Lady Day, when the Feast of the Annunciation of the Blessed Virgin is celebrated. There is a tradition that the Holy Mother wore a mary-golde in her bosom on that day, and a painter named Bartolomeo, who painted in 1430, represents her as clothed in a white robe covered with golden flowers, not unlike the marigold. The flower has also a place in heraldry. Margaret of Orleans, the maternal grandmother of King Henry IV, chose it as her armorial device, with the motto, "Je ne veux suivre que lui seul," meaning that she hoped her thoughts would always turn heavenward as the flower turned toward the sun. During the reign of King Henry VIII the flower was in high favor. Baskets of it were sent by gentlemen to the belles whom they admired. On special occasions, such as holidays and birthdays, wreaths of the smaller blossoms trimmed with heartsease were worn by ladies of the court to balls and fetes. In Mexico it is called the flower of death, and there is a tradition that it sprang from the ground stained with the life-blood of those natives who were slaughtered by the early Spanish invaders in their insatiable thirst for gold. It is used extensively to decorate the churches and for religious purposes, but there it is never made use of on festive occasions. In colonial days it was a cherished occupant of the front yards of our forefathers; but fashion, the autocratic dame, relegated it to the kitchen garden, where it bloomed in cheerful obscurity for many years, until the pre-Raphaelites resurrected it with the sunflower and some others. When it did not open about seven o'clock in the morning the gardeners knew that rain was likely. It now flourishes in a proud place of honor among those who wonder

FLOWER LORE AND LEGEND

how it could ever nave been thought common. In literature it is given a place more prominent than many flowers that would seem more deserving. This is particularly the case among the early English poets. Chaucer and Shakespeare frequently mention it. Chatterton, the boy prodigy of England, Browne, Herrick, and Constable all make use of it. Gay causes one of his shepherds to propound this riddle:

> "What is that flower that bears the Virgin's name,
> The richest metal joined with the same?"

George Withers, a contemporary of Shakespeare, in his quaint manner moralizes at some length upon its habits and attributes:

> "How duly, every morning, she displays
> Her open breast, when Phoebus spreads his rays;
> How she observes him, in his daily walk,
> Still bending tow'rds him her small slender stalk;
> How when he down declines, she droops and mourns,
> Bedewed, as 'twere with tears, till he returns."

Keats sings to it in his own inimitable verse:

> "Open afresh your round of starry folds,
> Ye ardent marigolds!
> Dry up the moisture from your golden lids,
> For great Apollo bids
> That in these days your praises should be sung
> On many harps, which he has lately strung;
> And when again your dewiness he kisses,
> Tell him, I have you in my world of blisses
> So haply when I rove in some far vale,
> His mighty voice may come upon the gale."
>   Keats, 'I Stood Tiptoe upon a Little Hill.'

FLOWER LORE AND LEGEND

THE ORCHID

A BELLE

"Who hung thy beauty on such slender stalk,
Thou glorious flower?
Mrs. Sigourney.
How comest thou hither? From what soil,
Where those that went before thee grew
Exempt from suffering, care and toil,
Clad by the sunbeams, fed with dew?
Tell me on what strange spot of ground
Thy rock-born kindred yet are found,
And I the carrier-dove will be
To bring them wondrous news of thee."

Montgomery.

Orchids have been called the elite among the flowers and undoubtedly lead in the fashionable world. The name, of Greek derivation, denotes the antiquity of the family and mythology gives an account of its origin. The satyrs were the deities of the woodlands, and the attendants of Dionysus or Bacchus. Orchis was the son of Pantellanus, the satyr, who was appointed to preside over certain bacchanalian feasts. At one of these he behaved so badly that the bacchanals seized him and literally tore him into a hundred pieces. His father begged them to spare him, but the only concession that they would make was that the mangled body should be changed into flowers, each piece taking a different shape and color. Therefore, the ancients called them satyrion, or flowers of the satyrs, who were supposed to feed upon the roots of these plants. To this was attributed many of the excesses which were characteristic of the attendants of Bacchus. Ten medicinal properties were accredited to the plant. The roots

FLOWER LORE AND LEGEND

grated and made into a paste were used in cases of external swellings. Boiled in water it was said to be healing to ulcers in the mouth. The juice, mixed with wine, was beneficial in cases of chronic intestinal trouble.

According to one of the most reliable authorities there are over twelve thousand varieties, the flowers of which, although differing widely within certain limits, are all formed upon one common plan. The differences, which are often extraordinary, and even grotesque, are brought about by what is known, in the botanical world, as cross-fertilization, which is effected by means of insects that carry the pollen from one flower to another. Darwin has written an exhaustive treatise upon this subject in which he says that a close examination of the habits of this plant will 'exalt the whole vegetable kingdom in the minds of most persons.' It is an illustration of the saying that 'Nature is much given to counterfeiting her own work,' that among its blossoms are found many striking imitations of animal life. The bee and the butterfly orchids are named from their likeness to these insects. The fly, the spider, the lizard, the bird's nest, the swan, and the monkey are all known to the experts. One species which blooms in Antrim is called anthropophora, or man orchid, because it resembles very exactly the body of a man wearing an extraordinarily large hat. A strangely beautiful type is a pure white blossom, called in South America el Spirito Santo, meaning the flower of the Holy Ghost. Many of the species belong to the class known as air plants. In the forests of South America, Mexico, and the East Indies, where the greater number of the more important plants are found, they grow from the trunks and branches of trees and in crevices of the rocks, without soil or direct supply of water. The seeds are so minute that they are blown about by the wind like dust.

This accounts for the singular places in which the plants have taken root. Although orchids are among the greatest curiosities in the whole range of the vegetable world, they have comparatively recently become well known and appreciated. It is about a century since they were introduced into the hot-houses of England, and they came into North America still later. When the first plants were sent by missionaries and army officers, they quickly attracted the attention of florists, and soon the orchid mania bade fair to rival the tulip mania, which shook financial Holland to its center in the seventeenth century. They are found in almost every part of the world, excepting where it is very cold, but grow most luxuriantly in the warmth and moisture of the tropics. Few who view these wonderful flowers with delight at exhibitions, or in orchid houses, know the difficulties under which the foreign specimens are obtained. Collectors, who are sent out by firms, societies, or individuals, are obliged to penetrate dense forests, exposed to danger from wild beasts, poisonous reptiles, and pestilential swamps. Often they go among savage tribes who resent the intrusion into their territory. One firm of English importers reported five collectors killed in as many months by the natives on the western slopes of the Himalayas. Many a rare specimen has been secured at the cost of a human life. London is the great orchid market of the world, and enormous prices are paid for single plants at auctions.

Ten thousand five hundred dollars is said to have been bid for a rare specimen. Much higher prices have been paid at private sales. Among noted collectors in England were Sir Rider Haggard, the Rothschilds, and Kitchener of Khartoum. Sir Joseph Chamberlain was the possessor of a magnificent collection in which he took great delight. After eighteen years of experimenting he had the satisfaction of producing an entirely new hybrid orchid, which he introduced to the floral world by a Latin name which means Chamberlain triumphant. It was his habit when in London to have two blossoms suitable for the purpose sent every morning from his Birmingham home and to appear daily in the House of Commons with one of them in his

FLOWER LORE AND LEGEND

coat, reserving the other for evening dress.

Among American collections, those of Mrs. G. W. Wilson of Philadelphia, H. S. Brown of Kirkwood, Me., and Oliver Ames at North Easton, Mass., probably rank as high as any. The White House conservatories have quite a good collection, which was recently increased by the gift of a large number from the Philippine Islands. A special car was chartered to transport them from San Francisco to Washington. In March, 1857, a new specimen of cypripedium, which is the botanical name of the genus, was exhibited in London. It had been sent by a druggist, named Simons, from Assam. The memoranda which should have accompanied it were lost and nothing definite was known about it. The blossom was very beautiful and florists tried in vain to reproduce it, but one of the peculiarities of the flowers is that they will not generate their own pollen. Hybridists were few in those days, methods not being well understood, and the variety gradually died out, until in 1876 it was classed as lost. In spite of the fact that special collectors were sent out to search every nook and corner of the world, and that, for twenty years, a standing reward of ten thousand dollars was offered to any one who would find a living specimen of the farrieneum variety, it remained undiscovered for almost fifty years. England had long desired to open commerce with Tibet, and while Russia and Japan were contending for Manchuria, English forces under Captain Younghusband were dispatched to penetrate the sacred precincts of Lhassa. Accompanying the troops was an engineer, named Seabright, who was also an amateur botanist. During one of his rambles he came upon the lost orchid. He sent the plants to Calcutta, where they were verified by Indian experts. In the spring of 1905, when one hundred and seventy-nine living plants were received in London, the reward was paid to him.

Ten varieties are natives of our country and are commonly known as the lady's-slipper, and sometimes, locally,

FLOWER LORE AND LEGEND

as the moccasin flower. Originally it was Our Lady's Slipper, referring to the Virgin. In 1893 the legislature of Minnesota passed an act naming the moccasin as the state flower.

In the pharmacopeia of the United States the orchid has an important place, but the remedies derived from it are directly opposite in their effect to those attributed to it by the ancients. Instead of a stimulant, it is now regarded as a sedative, and is used with beneficial effect in nervous and hysterical disorders, including epilepsy and tremors. It has none of the ill-effects of a narcotic. It is said to be the best American substitute for valerian. The vanilla bean, from which is produced the vanilla of commerce, is the seed of one variety. It is a climber and sometimes grows to a height of twenty or thirty feet, covering the tree upon which it finds support. It is cultivated principally in Mexico, South America, and Ceylon. Among the thousands of different species, it would be strange if there were not at least one with sacred associations.

There is an English variety which has dark purple spots on the leaves, and the tradition is that this plant grew upon Calvary and that the leaves were stained with the blood that flowed from the wounds of the crucified Savior. Another legend is that it grew in the garden of Gethsemane and that the drops of blood which our Lord sweated in His hour of agony fell upon the leaves and stained them. In some places the flower is still called Gethsemane. Shakespeare refers to it as long purples, or dead men's fingers. It is supposed to grow most luxuriantly in soil under which there are rich metal deposits. In China there is a secret league, known as the Society of the Golden Orchid. As the orchid has increased in popularity a special literature about it has grown up. There are magnificently illustrated monographs and periodicals entirely devoted to it; books and pamphlets on its cultivation, and catalogs of the different collectors. But although a flower of fashion, it does not seem to have appealed to the poets. Perhaps they have felt their inability to adequately extol its beauties.

Jean Ingelow tells us that the "purple orchid lasteth long," and Bayard Taylor wrote:

> "Around the pillars of the palm-tree bower
> The orchids cling, in rose and purple sphere"

While the peculiar shapes of some of the insect-like varieties are also referred to:

> "Think not to set the captive free,
> 'Tis but the picture of a bee,
> Yet wonder not that nature's power
> Should paint an insect in a flower,
> And stoop to means that bear in part
> Resemblance to imperfect art."

Snow, The Orchis,

FLOWER LORE AND LEGEND

THE VERBENA

YOU ENCHANT ME

"Sweet verbena! which being brushed against,
Will hold you three hours after by the smell,
In spite of long walks on the windy hills."

E. B. Browning, Aurora Leigh.

Verbena was an old Latin name for the flower that was later known throughout Europe as vervain. Both names mean a green bough. As an holy herb, it was held in the highest veneration by both Greeks and Romans, and marvelous qualities were attributed to it, not the least of which was the power of reconciling the bitterest enemies. It bore a prominent part in the official life of both nations. When the Romans felt that they had been treated discourteously by any of their neighbors, it was their custom to select four heralds from the members of the fetiales, whose duty it was to maintain the forms of international relationship, act as guardians of the public faith, and demand redress. These four selected one of their number to act as spokesman, who was sometimes the pater patratus or president of the college, but more generally he was merely a member and known as the verbenarius. Clothed in their priestly robes, wearing the insignia of their office, and preceded by the verbenarius, who in addition to his other vestments wore a white woolen band around his head, together with a wreath of the sacred verbena, gathered within the enclosure of the Capitoline Hill, and all bearing boughs of the same sacred plant, they advanced to the place where their negotiations were to be conducted. If war was decided upon, the verbenarius and his colleagues, wearing wreaths of verbena, approached the confines of the hostile territory. Throwing across the boundary a spear tipped with iron, and having a sprig of the holy herb bound upon its point, a solemn declaration of war was announced, and Jupiter was called upon to witness the justice of their cause. All treaties were approved by the college before they became effective and war was not declared until the demand for redress had first been made.

It was with water, in which this plant had been steeped, that the festal table of Jupiter was cleansed just before the feasts, which were prepared in the capitol by the septemviri in his honor. If the water was also used to sprinkle the banqueting couches before a feast, the merriment and hilarity was said to be thereby greatly promoted. Fletcher, in the Faithful Shepherdess, wrote:

> "And those light vervain, too, thou must go after,
> Provoking easy souls to mirth and laughter."

It was likewise used to cleanse houses in the belief that it kept away evil spirits. It was known as Juno's tears. A few leaves were worn on the person as a protection from harm. Romulus and Tatius, the Sabine, who ruled with him for seven years, are reported to have ordered that branches of the plant should be sent to them as a New Year's offering to insure their good fortune during the ensuing year. It was a favorite bridal flower. Roman brides were considered fortunate who wore a wreath which they gathered themselves. This tradition is doubtless the origin of a custom which has, until recently, been in vogue in some parts of Germany, where a bride is presented with a hat made of the blossoms, which she must wear during the ceremony. In Persia it was held in scarcely less veneration than among the Greeks and Romans. The priests of the temples of the sun always bore branches of it in their hands when they approached the altar, and the gathering of the plants was attended with much solemnity. It must take place at a time when neither the sun nor the moon was

FLOWER LORE AND LEGEND

visible. The roots were carefully cut below the surface and honey from the comb was poured into the place thus left vacant to appease the earth for robbing it of so precious a possession.

The magicians of the East also used it as a symbol of enchantment. They were responsible for the belief that if one smeared the body all over with the juice of the herb he would obtain whatever he might desire. He would also be enabled to curevany disease and reconcile those who were at enmity. Among the Druids of ancient Briton the plant was known by the name of vervain or holy herb. Almost the same ceremonies were observed in cutting it as were in vogue among the Persians, but with the restriction that the left hand only must be used. The leaves, stocks, and flowers were dried separately, and when mixed with wine were considered a certain cure for serpents' bites. At the time of the gathering of the mistletoe, a herald, clothed in white and bearing in his hands verbena branches, encircled by serpents, accompanied the druidic procession. When performing their daily task of feeding the never-dying fires in the temple, the priests spent half an hour in prayer, before the altar, holding in their hands branches of the sacred herb. One writer on antiquities states that the vervain was as especially holy to the priestesses as the mistletoe was to the priests. No one was allowed to touch it with the hand, and when it was gathered it must be at the full moon. A string was looped over the plant and then fastened to the toe of a young maid, who pulled until it was uprooted. The oldest druidess then threw a cloth over it and gathered it up. It was used in the sacred rites for offerings to the gods and medicinally as a cooling remedy.

During the Middle Ages the plant still retained its popularity. It was prescribed as a remedy for thirty different ailments, and for this reason was known as simples joy. In spite of the fact that it was used by witches for working their spells it was also used to combat the enchantments. Aubrey quotes the

FLOWER LORE AND LEGEND

old English proverb: "Vervain and dill hinder witches in their will." Dill is a flowering plant used in medicine. On Christmas Eve great bonfires were built, and the young men and maidens danced around them, wearing wreaths and garlands of vervain. Any young woman who gave to her lover a garland gathered and woven by her own hands insured his fidelity for at least all that year. Even now the superstition of its efficiency as a love philter has not entirely died out in some parts of England. A knot of vervain tied with white satin ribbon is still worn as a preventive of ague. French peasants gather the plant under certain phases of the moon, hoping with its magical assistance to charm those whose affection they desire. The Hungarian gypsies call it the lock-opening herb, saying that if a small incision is made in the palm of the hand, and a tiny piece of the leaf placed in the cut, the wound being allowed to heal over, one will be able to open all bolts and bars with a single touch. It is confidently asserted that therein lay the secret of the success of all the most famous brigands of old.

The plant is not without religious- association. As late as the seventeenth century it was known in Brittany as the herb-of-the-cross. The Reverend John White, in 1624, wrote of it:

> "Hallowed be thou, vervain, as thou growest in the ground,
> For on the Mount of Calvary thou first wert found."

Ben Jonson referred to the sacredness of the plant when he wrote: "Bring your garlands and with reverence place the vervain on the altar."

About 1826 the plant attracted the attention of English florists, who succeeded in obtaining several species of great beauty. Under the old Latin name of verbena it won great favor as a garden flower. Fourteen varieties are native in the United

FLOWER LORE AND LEGEND

States. In 1839, Robert Buiot, of Philadelphia, introduced the cultivation, and it was in the height of its popularity from 1848 to 1868, when it was beset with many destructive insects and diseases. When cultivated it includes all colors except yellow and pure blue, and some kinds are very fragrant. Other flowers have succeeded it in popularity.

It has never held a prominent place in literature. Virgil refers to it as a symbol of enchantment. The earlier English writers made frequent allusions both to its classical associations and to the superstitions connected with it during their own time. Dr. Johnson says that Satan has no power over a maiden who wears vervain and St. Johnswort about her. But elsewhere it appears that when it is gathered a cross must be first made over it and then a prayer said. Thereupon it is said to have been "crossed and blessed." Another old book says that to prepare a magic staff there must be put into a hollow place in it seven leaves of vervain, which must have been gathered on the eve of St. John the Baptist, and a stone of divers colors, which must be found in the nest of a bird called the lapwing. The hollow must be stopped up with boxwood. The staff, among other things, will preserve him who carries it from robbers, wild animals, and mad dogs.

It does not seem to have attracted modern writers.

"A wreath of vervain heralds wear,
Amongst our garlands named,
Being sent the dreadful news to bear
Offensive war proclaimed."

Drayton.

FLOWER LORE AND LEGEND

THE WATER LILY

ELOQUENCE - PURITY OF HEART

"In that dusk land of mystic dream,
Where dark Osiris sprung,
It bloomed beside his sacred stream,
While yet the world was young."

William Winter, A Lotus Flower.

"A flower delicious as the rose
And stately as a lily in her pride."

Under the name of the lotus, which some of our modern iconoclasts now declare to be historically incorrect, the water lily has drawn around it all the rich symbolism of the East. Long before Homeric days it was sacred, not only as a symbol, but was in itself an object of worship as the tree of life. According to Hindu theology, before the creation of the world, a great sea existed everywhere. Om, the Supreme, thought, and behold, Vishnu, the preserver, appeared floating in the water. He neither swam nor walked, but was borne by the gods upon nine golden lotus plants. From his body arose one of the blossoms in which was seated Brahma, the creator, who by his radiant countenance dispelled the gloom which hung over the waters, and by the power of his presence caused the earth to rise out of the sea. The paradise of the Hindu is described in the Mahabharata, the great Indian poem, as brilliant with gold and gems, and having many green valleys and beautiful lakes, upon the surface of which are myriads of these lilies, white, blue, and red, some of which have as many as a thousand petals. On a throne covered with them sits Om, the Supreme, and beside him is enthroned Lokamata, the mother of the world, who sitting upon a lily holds another in her hand. The sweet odor of the blossom is diffused all through the heavens. Buddha also appeared on earth, floating on the water in an enormous lotus and carrying another surmounted by a trident as his symbol. Many of the sacred images of India are represented as seated upon one, and it enters conspicuously into the decorations of their temples. In Egypt the plant was regarded as under the especial protection of the gods. It was dedicated to Osiris, the Apollo of the Egyptians. Dawn was typified by a youth dancing in a water lily. Like the Brahmans, their story of the creation was that a lily appeared upon the surface of the water and its leaves unfolded under the rays of Osiris, the sun-god. The ancient Egyptian always carried one of these lilies in his hand when approaching a place of worship, and offerings of them were placed in the tombs to pacify the anger of the gods. At festivals the walls of the banqueting halls were decorated, and great vases filled with them stood about the room and on the tables. Wreaths and necklaces, made from the stems and blossoms, were placed by the servants upon the heads and around the necks of the guests. While the lotus was reverenced by the inhabitants of Upper Egypt, in Lower Egypt the papyrus was the sacred plant.

The Indian variety was of a pinkish tinge, while that of Egypt was pure white. Both the seed and the root of the latter were used for food. The root was said to enclose a nut more delicate than the almond. The seeds were dried and then powdered into a flour, from which bread was made. In sowing the seeds they were enclosed in a ball of clay and thrown into the water. Some of the commentators suggest that this custom was referred to by Solomon in Ecclesiastes xi, 1, when he wrote: "Cast thy bread upon the waters, for thou shalt find it after many days." The Egyptians have many names for the plant, among them being one which means bride of the Nile. The surface of that great river, at the time of its rising, is covered with thousands of the white blossoms.

FLOWER LORE AND LEGEND

The Greeks regarded the water lily as the symbol of beauty and eloquence. According to their mythology, it owed its origin to a beautiful nymph, named Lotus, who fell deeply in love with Hercules. When he did not return her affection she died of a broken heart. Hebe, taking pity upon her, transformed her into the water lily. Long after, when Hercules went sailing with Jason in search of the golden fleece, he took with him Hylas, a youth whom he loved as his own son. When they reached the Hellespont they landed and prepared to rest. Hylas was sent to find a spring where they might get some water to drink. He found one near a pool of water, surrounded by green rushes and maiden-hair fern. The surface of the water was covered with white water lilies, each one being the home of a beautiful water-nymph. When Hylas put his pitcher down to dip up the water the maids all clung to his hand and drew him down into the depths of the pool. Just then one of the Argonauts shouted that the wind was fair for sailing. Hylas endeavored to go, but the water-nymphs held him fast. Hercules called him loudly three times, and the youth heard, but he could not answer, and his companions sailed mournfully away. Lotus was avenged, but the flowers were tinted with gold, the identifying color of an Argonaut, and the origin of the yellow water lily is thus accounted for. This is the source of the botanical name castalia nymphaea, the Latin word lutea being added for the yellow variety.

Some writers insist that the magic food upon which the lotus-eaters subsisted, and which caused whoever partook of it to forget everything in the dreamy languor of the present, was made from the seed of the Indian species. When Ulysses in his wanderings came to the enchanted island he sent three chosen men to explore the country. The islanders met them and entertained them hospitably; but after they had eaten of the food offered them they forgot country and friends, and refused to leave that happy land "where all things always seemed the same." Their leader, having had them bound hand and foot and forcibly brought on board ship, weighed anchor and hastily sailed away from the fatal shore.

The Japanese hold the plant in scarcely less veneration than their oriental neighbors. It is to them a constant symbol of purity and truth. As it is associated with death and the spirit world, the lily is considered inappropriate as a decoration for festivities. Certain sects believe that it is the flower of paradise, and when a death occurs on earth a new water lily appears on the surface of the lake in Nirvana, while the soul makes its entrance into the land of the blest at the unfolding of its own bud.

In China, the Shing-moo, or holy mother, is represented holding the lily in her hand. Few of their temples are without some representation of it. Abbe Hue, who was one of the first writers to give any account of the Chinese, said that the roots and seeds of the plant are a great resource in culinary preparations, and that in whatever manner it is dressed it is delicious and wholesome. The large leaves are made use of instead of paper for wrapping up parcels, The, Chinese poets are very fond of expatiating upon the beauty of the water lily gleaming in the moonlight, illumined by swarms of glow-worms and fire-flies. Isis, the goddess of fertility and abundance, was regarded by the adherents of the Hindu religion as the Queen of Heaven, and cakes made of corn and lotus seeds were favorite offerings to her. In the conspiracy which arose in British India, in 1857, and which resulted in the terrible Indian mutiny, these cakes accompanied by a lotus blossom were circulated among the Sepoys to notify them that they must rally to the standard of Buddha. Whatever other elements entered into that strife, whether the ambitions of princes, the desire for gain, or the intrigues of rival nations, the student of history will not fail to discern that a deeper one was the conflict between the lotus and the cross. The Order of the Lotus is conferred upon those who

FLOWER LORE AND LEGEND

have attained prominence in the administration of British India, and the collar of the order is ornamented with the heraldic rose of England alternating with the Indian lotus.

The beauty of the flower is thus emphasized by Shelley in the Passing Cloud:

> "Such luster water lilies throw
> Upon the brook that lies below,
> Lipping their blossoms with its flow,
> 'Twould make a landscape painter pine
> To win a hue to match with thine
> To make his martyr's mantle shine."

Dr. Halbertsma says that the old Frisians, who thought the water lily had mystical powers, also believed that if a person fell with one in his hand he would become subject to fits. In several countries it was regarded as an antidote where a person had taken a love potion. The Wallachians have a superstition that every flower has a soul, and they say that the lily is the sinless flower, and when it dies it blossoms again at the doors of heaven, where it judges the souls of the other flowers as they arrive, and solemnly demands of each flower a strict account of the use it has made of its perfume. An Eastern song tells the tale of a star that looked down upon a water lily as the sun stepped into the golden sea and loved her. But she was too sleepy to care much about his fond words, and she tightly closed the great thick leaves about her beauty. He could not see her in the daytime, because of the brightness of the sun, and it was only at evening that he could smile upon her, but then she was too tired to respond. At last his heart burst and he shot from the sky into the pond. For a moment the lily was startled and opened her leaves to look at the bright glare. But the falling star plunged into the water and his light and beauty were extinguished forever.

FLOWER LORE AND LEGEND

In our country, also, legends of the pond lily originated. Many, many years ago, when the Indians alone possessed the American wilderness, a band of warriors were encamped on the shore of a lake. At night, as they sat and smoked their pipes, they watched the stars, for in them they believed dwelt the good who had been taken away by the Great Spirit. Once they saw a star that seemed brighter and nearer than any of the others. A council of their wise men was called to ascertain the meaning of this wonder. Some thought that it was an omen of evil; others that it was a messenger of good. A whole moon passed and the mystery remained unsolved. One night a young brave dreamed that a radiant maiden stood beside him and said: "I love your land, its lakes and its mountains, its birds and its flowers, and I have left my sisters to dwell among you. Ask your people where I can live and what form I shall take to be loved of all." At dawn the warriors were summoned to the council lodge, and the young brave reported his dream. Three of the wisest were chosen to welcome the stranger. They were surprised to find that as they went toward the star it seemed to advance nearer and nearer to meet them, until it was almost within their reach. They offered a pipe of peace filled with fragrant herbs, and it was taken by unseen hands. As they returned, the star followed, and hovered over the camp until dawn. That night the maiden again appeared to the young brave to know what form she should take and where she should live. Numerous places were suggested, but at last it was decided to leave it to the maiden to choose for herself.

At first she chose a white rose on the mountain, but no one could see her. Then she selected a prairie flower, but the hoof of the buffalo crushed her to earth. Then she passed into a honeysuckle on the cliff, but the children could not reach her. At last the star said: "I know where I will go. I will be safe and I can watch the canoes as they come and go, and the children can play with me." So saying, she dropped gently into the cool water of

FLOWER LORE AND LEGEND

the lake, and the next morning thousands of white pond lilies were blooming there. The Indians called them wah-be-gwan-nee, meaning the white flower. Another account of the origin of these lilies comes from the Caranac tribe. It was summer. All the spring the young brave chief, Wayotah, or the blazing sun, with his warriors had been away fighting with a neighboring tribe, but they had returned victorious to their camp on the shore of the lake of the reflected stars. There was wild feasting and revelry to welcome them home. Every one was joyous, save one, and she should have been the happiest of all, for in one week she was to be the bride of the victorious chief. Oseetah, which means the bird, or the sweet singer of the tribe, had vowed a vow, that no one knew of save the Great Spirit, and she was sad. Silently she withdrew from the throng, and slipping into her canoe paddled along the shore of the lake. But her lover had seen her, and, running to the shore, sprang into his canoe to follow. On they went, until beaching her canoe, she climbed up to the top of a high cliff. She called to her lover not to follow, but he either did not, or would not, understand. On he came climbing after her to find out what was the matter and to persuade her to go back with him. Perceiving that she could not stop him, Oseetah turned her face to the sky and leaped from the cliff into the lake below. The chief sprang in after her, and swam with giant strokes, searching everywhere for her, but in vain. She was not to be found, and after a while he went sadly back to his people. The feasting was changed into mourning, for the maiden was loved by all.

The next day a stranger came to the Indian village, holding in his hand a new flower. No Indian had ever seen one like it, and much wonder was expressed. Their surprise was still greater when he told them in the lake of the reflected stars there were many more just like it. Hurriedly they went to see for themselves, and sure enough, there were hundreds of great, white water lilies floating on the water. While they were gazing a man appeared, dressed in flowing robes, and he told them that

FLOWER LORE AND LEGEND

because Oseetah had been true to her vow the Great Spirit had given her a new form. The white petals were for her goodness, the yellow center for her faith, and the green leaves a symbol that she should live forever. Every morning she would open to the sun as he rose, and close when he sank beneath the horizon in the evening. And so to the Indian the pond lily is the emblem of good faith.

In Germany it is believed that the Undines, or water spirits, make their homes in the heart of the water lilies. As the night comes on the petals of the flowers close tightly, shutting them in, and then slowly sink down into the water to rise and open in all their beauty with the morning sun. There is a story of a German knight, who loved one of these beautiful nymphs and made her his wife. Soon after the marriage he wanted to take his lady out on the water in a boat. She begged him not to go, but he laughed at her fears. Tearfully she slipped into the boat with him. They had not gone far when hundreds of little hands dragged the boat and its occupants under the water. The next morning two lilies, larger and more beautiful than the others, appeared near where the boat had gone down.

The most wonderful variety of the water lily in the world is the Victoria regia. It was introduced into England from South America about 1850 and Professor Lindley, who has written an exhaustive monograph treating of it and its culture, has named it after England's great and good Queen. The blossoms are enormous, while the leaves sometimes measure nine feet across and can bear up a man. The plant is night blooming. The first evening that it opens the blossom is white and the odor is almost oppressive. On the second day when it unfolds it is pink. This remarkable flower is grown in many public and private gardens in the United States.

There has been almost as much attention paid in

FLOWER LORE AND LEGEND

literature to the water lily as to the rose and the violet. Under the name of the lotus, ancient authors wrote of its mystical qualities and religious symbolism, and in later days as an emblem of purity and beauty it has been a favorite with writers of both poetry and prose. Thoreau's chapter on water lilies is cooling to the most fevered mind. Heine, Moore, Shelley, and Wordsworth have all paid their tribute to the mystic flower. A recent laureate of England chose it as an exquisite emblem of affection.

> "Now folds the lily all her sweetness up
> And slips into the bosom of the lake;
> So fold thyself, my dearest, thou, and slip
> Into my bosom, and be lost in me."

Tennyson, The Princess.

> "Those virgin lilies all the night
> Bathing their beauties in the lake,
> That they may rise more fresh and bright,
> When their beloved sun's awake."

Thomas Moore, Paradise and the Peri.

FLOWER LORE AND LEGEND

THE POPPY

CONSOLATION - OBLIVION

"Yonder poppies full of scorn,
Proudly wave above the corn."

Walter Thornbury.

"Bring poppies for the weary mind
That saddens in a senseless din."

William Winter.

When Proserpina was carried away by Pluto, her mother, Ceres, who clothes the earth with verdure and protects the flowers and crops, despaired of ever seeing her again. Her grief was so great that she could neither sleep nor eat, and she besought Flora, the goddess of the flowers, to help her. As all vegetation was in a fair way to be destroyed, Flora appealed to Somnus, one of the gods, and with his aid created a flower which possessed narcotic qualities. After partaking of a liquid distilled from the seed of this plant, Ceres fell into a deep sleep, during which all the plants, grasses, and flowers were refreshed. According to the traditions of the ancient Greeks this was the origin of the poppy. Ceres adopted the plant for her own, and poppy seeds were planted with the corn and wheat to propitiate the goddess of agriculture and to prevent her from destroying the crops should she become angered. The red variety is called popaver rhceas and corn rose. Ceres is represented by artists as crowned with poppies and bearded wheat. A poet once wrote:

"Visions aye are on us,
Unto eyes of power;

FLOWER LORE AND LEGEND

> Pluto's always setting sun,
> And Proserpina's bower."

According to an Indian legend, there lived on the banks of the Ganges an ancient dervish, who had a pet mouse of which he was so fond that he endowed it with the gift of speech. But a cat who lived in the vicinity kept the mouse in such a state of terror that the sage changed it into a dog. The animal was still discontented and was transformed to an ape, then to a boar, then to an elephant, and finally into a beautiful maiden, whom the dervish named Postomani or poppy-seed. One day, as she was in the garden, the King passed, and being attracted by her beauty later returned and insisted upon knowing her name and parentage. She told him that she was a Princess, who had been left in the care of the wise man when a child. The King was so much in love that he did not stop to question the truth of her story, and insisted upon being married at once by the dervish, They lived happily until one day she was standing by a well, and becoming dizzy fell in and was drowned. In order to reconcile the King to her loss, the dervish, telling him that she was not of royal birth, but had been a mouse, a dog, an ape, and other animals, gave directions that the well should be filled up with earth without removing the body, and foretold that out of her grave a plant should grow, from which would be obtained a drug, and whoever should use this drug would be endowed with one quality of each of the animals into which she had been transformed. He should be mischievous like the mouse, savage like the dog, filthy like the ape, wild like the boar, and slow like the elephant. This is the effect of the drug to this day.

The narcotic qualities of the plant were very early recognized by the ancients. Hypnos, the god of sleep, and Thanatos, the god of death, were both represented in art as holding poppies in their hands. A modern poet wrote:

FLOWER LORE AND LEGEND

"For happy hours the rose will blow.
The poppy hath a charm for pain and woe."

The youths and maidens of both Greece and Rome used its petals to test the sincerity of their loves. One was placed in the palm of the left hand, and if, upon being smartly struck with the right hand, it snapped with a sharp sound, the loved one was faithful. Otherwise, if it failed to make any noise. Theocritus alludes to this custom:

"By a prophetic poppy leaf, I found
Your changed affection, for it gave no sound."

The North American Indians have few legends associated with flowers, but the poppy is one of the exceptions. In very early times, before the white man had set his foot in the new world, there was a famine in the land. When winter came and the cold winds blew, all vegetation was frozen and the natives died by the hundreds, until there was left only the Chief Manona and his young squaw. Together they started out to find a place of refuge. Crossing the frozen rivers and climbing the snow-capped mountains they prayed all the time to the Great Spirit for help. At last they were heard. The wind ceased to blow, the ice and snow melted, and everywhere there came forth bright red flowers, which brought warmth and plenty to the land. Thus the fire-flower is still dear to the heart of the Indian. In our land the poppy is chiefly an ornament, but in India, China, and Persia it is of great commercial value. The poppy fields of China are as famed as the wheat fields of the Dakotas. One writer says: "For five days we traveled through fields of poppies." It is being cultivated at the expense of rice, which is double the price it was ten years ago. In the middle of the nineteenth century the poppy was indirectly the cause of a war between England and China, known as the opium war, which was terminated in August, 1842, by the celebrated Nanking Treaty, and resulted in the opening of

FLOWER LORE AND LEGEND

China, which before had been closed, to the people of the world. Medicinally it is used as a sedative and as an anodyne. The blossoms are red, white, yellow, and sometimes so purple that they are said to be black. There is a bee which is known as the upholsterer because it lines its nest with poppy petals. Perhaps this serves to keep the young bees quiet until they are old enough to fly. When the Archduke Maximilian and his beautiful wife, the unfortunate Carlotta, crossed the sea to establish an empire in Mexico, they wished to institute an order corresponding to the Legion of Honor in France and to that of the Garter in England. The Empress decided that the color of the ribbon should be bright red. Napoleon III objected, as red was the color of the Legion, but Carlotta, enclosing a poppy petal in a letter, wrote him that the order of Nature antedated the Legion of Honor, and that she should copy that.

In colonial days the children were not permitted to play with toys on the Sabbath. But the little girls made dolls with red petticoats from the poppies. Perhaps this was a survival of a very old custom, as the name is derived from the French word poupee, which means doll or rag baby. Wreaths of poppies have long been popular. Ben Jonson refers to the use of horned poppies by witches. The oil which is made from the opium poppy is used for food and lighting purposes. Its color is golden. French soapmakers find it useful. California was the first state to adopt a flower emblem, and the popular choice fell upon the golden poppy, which was a most appropriate selection, as the flower grows wild in great profusion in all parts of the state. In 1849, when the rush for gold first began in the western Eldorado, the Indians believed that the leaves of the Great Spirit's flower, dropping year after year, sank into the earth and were changed into the yellow metal that the white man held so precious. The Spanish name of the golden poppy is copa de oro, meaning cup of gold, and one of the poets of California has written of it:

FLOWER LORE AND LEGEND

"Copa de oro, chalice of gold,
Who fashioned thee so daintily; whose hand did hold
The graver that chased thy rounded brim?
Old Tubal Cain could strive in vain to equal him."

The poppy is more of a favorite with modern writers than with the ancients. Perhaps this may be accounted for by the fact that in olden times the flower was associated with death. It is a frail blossom. Robert Burns refers to this:

"Pleasures are like poppies spread,
You seize the flower, the bloom is shed."

Shakespeare mentions it once when Iago, in Othello, refers to the narcotic properties of the plant. Keats makes numerous references to it, and Bayard Taylor has written rather sadly about it:

"We are slumbering poppies,
Lords of Lethe downs,
Some awake, and some asleep,
Sleeping in our crowns.
What perchance our dreams may know,
Let our serious beauty show."

Leigh Hunt, Songs and Chorus of the Flowers.

FLOWER LORE AND LEGEND

THE IRIS

A MESSAGE

"Oh flower-de-luce, bloom on, and let the river
Linger to kiss thy feet!
Oh flower of song, bloom on, and make forever
The world more fair and sweet!"

Longfellow, Flower-de-luce.

In ancient myth, Iris, the sister of the harpies and goddess of the storm, was represented by the rainbow. She was as swift as the wind, had wings of gold, and was employed by Juno for her especial messenger, as Mercury was the messenger of Jupiter. She carried messages unto the ends of the earth and even into the depths of the sea. By some of the Greek poets she is called a virgin goddess. One day the flowers all assembled at the invitation of Juno to celebrate the birthday of Iris. They all came in their prettiest dresses and were having a fine time when three new sister flowers were seen approaching, dressed in gowns of red, yellow, and purple, and wearing gorgeous jewels, but no one knew who they were. As they were without names, they were christened Iris, because they wore the colors of the rainbow, and thus it is that they bear the name of the messenger of the gods. There are more than one hundred and seventy different varieties of the plant and they grow in almost every country on the earth. The blue flag is a native of the United States and the yellow of Europe and Asia. Many fossil varieties now unknown are found in the rocks.

As one of the duties of Mercury was to conduct the souls of dead men to their final resting place, so Iris performed the same duty for the women. The Greeks used the purple variety to

FLOWER LORE AND LEGEND

decorate the graves of the women. The Egyptians introduced the flower in their architecture. As the symbol of eloquence and power, it was placed upon the brow of the sphinx and upon the scepters of their rulers. In ancient Babylon and Assyria it was recognized as one of the symbols of royalty. It was also esteemed highly for medicinal purposes. The roots, which had many of the properties of honey, were used in the preparation of forty-one different remedies. The plant attached to the body of an infant was supposed to correct all the disorders that arise from teething.

A syrup made from the root was said to cure coughs and inflammation of the throat. Mixed with vinegar, the essence was good for diseases of the liver. Applied externally, the plant was a cure for the bites of serpents and scorpions. A powder made from the root and mixed with honey was used as a splint for broken bones. Used dry it was beneficial in cases of scrofulous sores. The person gathering it must at the time name the patient and the disease for which it was to be used. A Roman naturalist mentions a crime practiced by some herbalists. When they thought they had not been paid enough they kept a portion of it and by burying it in the same place, from which they obtained it, a recurrence of the illness and consequent retention of their services were assured. An exquisite perfume was made from some varieties and it was in much demand among women of fashion. A perfumed oil, which was a valued addition to the toilet, was also obtained from it. The iris is the national flower of France, where it was first called Heur-de-lys. There are several legends in regard to its adoption. According to heraldic traditions, the ancient Franks, at a proclamation of the King, were accustomed to place in his hand a reed of the flag in blossom, and the later rulers are represented with their scepters ornamented with the same flower. Another legend is traced to the sixth century When Clotilda, the wife of Clovis, endeavored by prayers and good deeds to bring about the conversion of her warlike husband to Christianity, for a long time he resisted her

FLOWER LORE AND LEGEND

efforts. At length, having led his army against the Huns and being in danger of defeat, he called for assistance upon the God whom his wife worshiped. The tide of battle turned. He won a complete victory, and upon his return was baptized in the Christian faith. The night after his baptism an angel appeared to a holy hermit who dwelt near the castle and gave him a beautiful blue shield emblazoned with three golden fleurs-de-lys, which he bade the hermit take to the Queen to give to her husband.

The device of Clovis had heretofore been three black toads. The banner of Charlemagne is also said to have been blue decorated with golden fleurs-de-lys. A later tradition is that when Louis VII was about to start on his crusade to the Holy Land the white banner of the French Crusaders was found one morning covered with purple fleurs-de-lys. Louis regarded it as an evidence of the Divine approval, and adopted it as the emblem of France, and had it engraved upon his signet ring. The soldiers called the flower fleur-de-Louis, which later was contracted into fleur-de-luce, and still later into the present form, 'fleur-de-lys.' It was also incorporated into the arms of France and used in the decoration of the crown itself. Charles VI reduced the number of fleurs-de-lys used in emblazoning the French arms to three, supposedly in recognition of the Holy Trinity. Edward III claimed France as belonging to the English Crown and added the flower to the English coat-of-arms. It took many bloody battles to make the English renounce this claim, but at last, in 1801, the flower disappeared from the English shield. During the French revolution the fleur-delys was proscribed, and any one wearing it or having it in his possession was put to death. Where it was conspicuous in decoration or sculpture it was destroyed by the frenzied mob. Upon the base of the statue of Jeanne d'Arc in Rouen are sculptured fleurs-de-lys, with this inscription:

"Beneath the maiden's sword,
The lilies safely bloom."

FLOWER LORE AND LEGEND

After 1789 the tri-color became the national emblem. The Japanese, with their extravagant love for flowers, celebrate a flower festival every month. The fete of the iris, or hana-shoby, occurs in June. In contrast to the riotous carnival of the cherry blossom this event is a very dignified garden party. They have brought the flower to a perfection that the French never dreamed of. Purple, yellow, and white are the principal colors, and also some shades of blue. The most important display is at Horokiri, near Tokio, where the plants are arranged to produce a wonderful color effect. During the celebration the hot water in the public bathhouses is perfumed with iris root and the public conveyances are decorated with garlands of the flowers. It has long been the custom for the Japanese, on the fifth day of June, to hang bunches of sweet flag, which is a wild iris, under the eaves of their houses to warn off evil spirits and to prevent misfortune coming to their homes. Sometimes beds of it are planted on the thatched roofs of the cottages to ward off pestilence. This is accounted for because once there was a famine in Japan, and no one was allowed to plant anything in the ground that could not be used as food. The powdered root of the plant was applied by Japanese women as a cosmetic and as a powder to whiten their faces, so the little ladies all planted gardens of it on the roofs of their houses, and in many of the country places they are still there.

They make it a custom to send flowers upon all occasions, and the iris is in great demand for events requiring congratulations, except at weddings, when it is undesirable on account of the purple color. Their literature has many references to the flower. One of their poets wrote:

> "The iris grown between my house and the neighbors
> Is just burnishing in its deepest color and glory,
> I wish that some one would come and see it
> Before it withers away, and returns to the dust."

FLOWER LORE AND LEGEND

The French poets have naturally made their national flower a frequent theme for verse, and the earlier English writers have numerous references to it. Chaucer and Ben Jonson both seem to have been familiar with it. As the fleur-de-lys was an emblem of royalty, it came to be attributed to our Savior. In a carol which is known to have been sung before 1526 the origin of the flower is thus told:

> "For His love that bought us all dear,
> Listen, lordings, that be here,
> And I will tell you in fere
> Whereof came the fleur-de-lys.
> On Christmas night, when it was cold,
> Our Lady lay among beasts bold,
> And there she bare Jesu, Joseph told,
> And thereof came the fleur-de-lys.
> Sing we all for time it is;
> Mary hath borne the fleur-de-lys."

'In fere' as thus used means 'all together.' Spenser includes it in his Shepherd's Calendar. Shakespeare often refers to it in his historical plays, while Milton numbers it with the flowers of Paradise:

> "Iris all hues, roses, and jassamin,
> Reared high their heads and wrought mosaic."

It grows in wet or damp soil. Shelley refers to this when he says:

> "And nearer to the river's trembling edge
> There grew broad flag flowers, purple prankt with white."

As a religious symbol the iris is sacred to the Virgin

FLOWER LORE AND LEGEND

Mary. There was once a knight who was not learned, but who was most devout. He never could remember more than two words of the Latin prayer to the Holy Mother. These words were Ave Maria, and he repeated them over and over, night and day, until at last he died and was buried in the chapel-yard of a convent near which he lived. After a while a strange flower grew on his grave, a fleur-de-lys, which bore on every blossom in golden letters the words Ave Maria. The monks, who had held him in contempt during his life, because of his ignorance, opened the grave and were surprised to find the root of the plant resting on the lips of the holy knight, whose body lay in the grave:

> "It blooms in May and June,
> O'er her tall blades
> The crested fleur-de-lys,
> Like blue-eyed Pallas,
> Towers erect and free."

Holmes, Spring.

FLOWER LORE AND LEGEND

THE THISTLE

AUSTERITY – INDEPENDENCE - RETALIATION

> "The rose may bloom for England;
> The lily for France unfold;
> Ireland may have her shamrock;
> Scotland has the thistle bold."

Edna Dean Proctor.

> "Proud thistle, emblem dear to Scotland's sons,
> Begirt with threatening points, strong in defense,
> Unwilling to assault."

The thistle of Scotland is said to be the oldest national flower on record, and tradition traces its adoption to the reign of Alexander III and the battle of Largs. In the year 1263 there was war between the Danes and the Scots, and the army of the northmen under King Haakon succeeded in landing unobserved on the coast of Scotland near the mouth of the Clyde, not far from where Alexander's army was encamped. The Danes regarded it as contrary to the ethics of warfare to attack an enemy at night, but on this occasion the temptation was too great and they deviated from their rule. They crept stealthily toward the Scottish camp and almost accomplished their purpose. Victory seemed within their grasp, when one of the barefooted soldiers trod upon a thistle. Its prickles caused him to utter a sharp cry of pain and the alarm was given. The Scotch warriors seized their weapons and proceeded to drive the invaders from their shore with great slaughter. Since that time, it is stated, the thistle has been the national emblem of Scotland.

Another account of its adoption is of a very different

FLOWER LORE AND LEGEND

character. About the middle of the fifteenth century a company of stern-faced, bearded men met in the old council chamber at Edinburgh, and the occasion of that meeting was to discuss the advisability of substituting the thistle for the figure of St. Andrew on their national banner. f The proceedings of the council were secret, but soon after the thistle appeared upon every Scottish banner. The national motto might have been adopted with equal appropriateness on either of these occasions: "Nemo me impune lacessit." The polite reading of this is, "No man attacks me without being punished" but the more simple translation of earlier days was, "Touch me who dares!" while the original motto is supposed to have been, "Wha dare meddle wi' me?" Another inscription which sometimes accompanies the Scottish emblem reads: "Ce que Dieu garde, est bien garde"; "That which God guards is well guarded."

The thistle appeared officially for the first time during the reign of James II, who had it placed upon the coinage of the kingdom and adopted it as his personal badge. It also appeared upon the coins of the reign of James IV, Mary Stuart, James V, and James VI. The thistle merke was a silver shilling. The thistle dollar was a double merke. The thistle crown was a gold dollar. Each took its name from the emblem on it. The Most Ancient Order of the Thistle, which the Scots claim antedates the Order of the Garter, was founded by James V of Scotland. It consisted of the sovereign and twelve knights in memory of our Lord and the Apostles. It has for its insignia the blossom and leaves of a thistle in gold, together with the national motto. During the reign of Queen Anne it pleased her to bestow upon the great Scotchman, the Duke of Hamilton, the Order of the Garter. The nobleman refused it unless he should also be allowed to wear the Order of the Thistle, saying that he would never lay down the thistle to make way for the rose, and reminding her that Her Majesty's father, James II of England, had bestowed the Scottish honor upon him. The Queen not only permitted him to wear both orders, but from that time wore them herself. The number in the order had then dwindled to eight, but she restored it to twelve. The coat-of-arms of the national bank of Scotland, granted in 1826, bears a figure of St. Andrew, the patron saint of Scotland, carrying his cross before him, surrounded by a border of thistles.

The first allusion to it as the Scottish emblem is by Dunbar in his poem, The Thistle and the Rois, written in 1501 on the marriage of James IV to Margaret Tudor. Since then the poets of Scotland have always been ready to pay it homage and those of other countries generally have not ventured to do otherwise. James Hogg wrote:

> "Up wi' the flowers o' Scotland,
> The emblem o' the free;
> Their guardians for a thousand years
> Their guardians still we'll be.
> A foe had better brave the de'il
> Within his reeky cell,
> Than our thistle's purple bonnet
> Or our bonny heather bell."

There has been some controversy as to which variety of the plant was originally selected as the Scottish emblem, but the common cotton thistle, with its purple flower, is generally accepted as the true one. The family is large and widely diversified. The blossoms are purple, yellow, and white. In France, Germany, and Spain there grows a variety known as the carline thistle. It is very large and the country folk hang it outside their cottage doors as a barometer. Before a rain the blossom invariably closes, and when the storm is nearly over it gradually opens. It derived its name from its association with Charlemagne. On one occasion, as the story is told, when the Emperor was engaged in war a plague broke out among his soldiers, many of whom died. He prayed to God for help and that

FLOWER LORE AND LEGEND

night an angel appeared to him and shot an arrow from a crossbow, telling him that on the spot where the arrow fell he would find a plant, the root of which was the best antidote for the disease. The Emperor followed the direction indicated and found a large thistle with an arrow fastened in its branches.

The instructions thus received resulted most successfully. In Tartary there is a species which grows so large that the natives build their huts in its shade. As autumn approaches the stem decays and the blossom dries into a feather-ball, which is driven over the plains by the wind. It is called the windwitch, and it is said that no one has ever been known to catch one; but this is not true of the Canada thistle, which resembles it. Still another variety is Our Lady's thistle. It is so called on account of the white spots on the leaves. The legend is that one day the Blessed Virgin sat down in the field to nurse the Child Jesus and some of the milk fell upon a thistle growing near by, causing the leaves to assume their peculiar coloring.

Mary, Queen of Scots, hoped to make it the thistle of Scotland and caused it to be planted on the cliffs surrounding the castle of Dumbarton. The plant has several medicinal properties. It is claimed that when gathered before it blossoms and the leaves and stem are bruised, the juice applied to the scalp will make the hair grow. Mixed with vinegar, it was used to heal leprous sores. It was also said to be a remedy for disorders of the stomach. The roots were boiled and used for food. Pliny, commenting upon this, said: "No four-footed animal save the ass will eat it." Finches, however, feed upon the blossoms and the seeds. Marlowe and Chapman in Hero and Leander, speak of this:

> "Two sweet birds surnamed th' acanthides,
> Which we call thistle warps, that near no seas
> Dare ever come, but still in couples fly,

FLOWER LORE AND LEGEND

And feed on thistle tops to testify
The hardness of their first life in the last."

It had a place among the mystical plants, as sacred to Thor. Carried about the person it was said to protect the bearer from all evil and especially lightning. In some places thistles were placed on the first corn that ripened to drive away evil spirits from the fields. In England there was an old superstition that if a maiden wished to find out which of several suitors loved her the best she must take the heads of thistles, cut off their points, give each flower the name of a person, and put them under her pillow. The one that put forth a new sprout loved her the best. It was a lucky omen to dream of being surrounded by thistles. The dreamer in a short time was sure to hear some good news.

There is an old saying that first loves float from the memory like thistledown in a breeze. In a wild, barren spot near Mecklenburg, where a murder was once committed, there grew a strangely form a variety. Every day at noon it appeared with what looked like human arms, hands, and head. Daily a new head was produced until twelve different ones had appeared, when the plant mysteriously disappeared and a new one came in its place. Every one avoided the spot. One day a shepherd declared that he was not afraid, and taking his staff started to pass the weird plant. The staff immediately turned to tinder and both his arms were paralyzed. This story is told by Mannhardt, the German mythologist, who died in 1880. The thistle is not a popular plant outside of Scotland, and farmers all over the world hold it in great disfavor on account of the rapidity with which it spreads and the difficulty in uprooting. It is really a weed and grows in poor soil. The earliest mention of it in literature is in Genesis, chapter iii, verse 18, where it is made a part of the primal curse. There are eight succeeding references to it in the Scriptures, in each of which it is mentioned as something to be

FLOWER LORE AND LEGEND

deplored. Cowper, in the Task, said:

> "The land once lean
> Or fertile only in its own disgrace
> Exults to see its thistly curse repealed."

Modern references, aside from agricultural works, emphasize its more admirable qualities.

> "A thistle grew in a sluggish croft,
> Rough and rank with a thorny growth,
> With its spotted leaves and its purple flower,
> (Blossoms of sin, blooms of sloth),
> Slowly it ripened its baneful seeds,
> And away they scattered in swift gray showers,
> But every seed was cobweb winged,
> And they spread o'er a hundred miles of land;
> Tis centuries now since they first took flight,
> In that careless, gay, and mischievous band,
> Yet still they are blooming and ripening fast
> And spreading their evil by day and night."

Anon, The Lie.

FLOWER LORE AND LEGEND

THE COLUMBINE

DESERTION - INCONSTANCY

"Skirting the rocks at the forest edge
With a running flame from ledge to ledge,
Or swaying deeper in shadowy glooms,
A smouldering fire in her dusky blooms;
Bronzed and molded by wind and sun,
Maddening, gladdening every one
With gipsy beauty full and fine,
A health to the crimson columbine!"

The columbine belongs to the crowfoot family, and is one of about thirty varieties scattered throughout North America and Great Britain. It flourishes in July and August. The generic name of the flower is aquilegia, about the derivation of which there has been much discussion, some asserting that it is from the Latin meaning the eagle, and that it was given to the plant on account of the spurs on the blossom that are bent somewhat like the talons of that lordly bird. Others insist that it is from the words aqua, which means water, and ligo, meaning to collect, because the petals of the blossom are funnel-shaped, as if intended to hold water. This intention, however, is frustrated by the position of the flowers, as they hang mouth downward. The European blossom is not as graceful as its American sisters, being shorter and stouter; nor is it as brilliant in color. Another name which was once used was culverwort, which means dove-plant, and it was so called because after removing the outer petals those remaining resembled a cluster of doves eating from the same dish. The word columbine comes from the Latin columba, which means a dove. It used to be applied to persons of a dove-like nature. The flower was sometimes known as 'herb of the lion,' from the belief that it was the favorite of the king of

FLOWER LORE AND LEGEND

beasts. The name was dear to the children of a generation ago through its association with the Christmas pantomime, which was an elaborate feature of the English holiday season, and was brought to this country occasionally by some enterprising manager. The play was adapted from an old fairy tale. There was a cross old guardian, whose beautiful ward had two lovers, one a fine, handsome young man whom she preferred, the other a rakish old fop whose wealth had attracted her guardian. A meddlesome servant made all sorts of trouble for the young people, and just at the moment when the young girl was about to be married to the suitor whom she despised a good fairy appeared and changed everything and everybody. The young girl was transformed into a wonderful creature called Columbine, and the young lover into Harlequin; the old curmudgeon into Pantaloon, and the mischievous servant into a clown. Columbine and Harlequin had a most exciting time trying to escape from their pursuers. Finally the good fairy appeared again and straightened everything. The aged suitor disappeared, the guardian gave his blessing, and the lovers skipped happily through life. Jones Very wrote:

> "The morning's blush, she made it thine.
> The morn's sweet breath, she gave it thee.
> And in thy look, my Columbine,
> Each fond-remembered spot she bade me see."

Not only in fairy-lore, but also in heraldry the blossom has played an important part. During the reign of Henry IV it was combined with the red rose as a badge of the royal house of Lancaster, and long before that it had appeared in company with the historic broom-flower, on the official arms of the Plantagenets. In Latin the broom was planta genista and in French plante-genet. From this that great family name was derived. In a bill presented by a painter in connection with the funeral ceremonies of Baron Grey of Vitten is found this

FLOWER LORE AND LEGEND

item; "His creste, a bunch of collobyns, blue, with stalk vert."

The arms of Cadman bore a spray of the blue columbine, and it appeared also on the shield of a coat-of-arms granted to a Bohemian knight in 1701. Examples of early design show that both the flower and the leaf were favorite motives in decoration. It is found employed as a border upon an illuminated manuscript as early as the fifteenth century. William Morris used it repeatedly as a leading feature of his wonderful designs, but he says, "Choose the old single columbine where the doves are unmistakable and distinct."

American artists are just beginning to appreciate its decorative possibilities. Recently it came prominently to the foreground. The rumor that a memorial was about to be presented to Congress asking that the mountain laurel be recognized as our national floral emblem started a controversy for floral supremacy beside which the Wars of the Roses bade fair to dwindle into insignificance. At the time of the Columbian Exposition in Chicago the National Floral Emblem Society of America was organized. Its object was to obtain a genuine expression of the will of the people which might lead to the adoption of a national flower. Committees were appointed in different parts of the country, and as a result of this activity a National Flower Convention was called by Governor Cross of North Carolina to be held at Asheville, in October, 1896, for the purpose of recommending a suitable flower to Congress for adoption as the official emblem. Delegates appointed by the Governors of their respective states, including many experts in botany and horticulture, as well as literature and art, met at the appointed time, and the merits and demerits of the different floral candidates were thoroughly discussed. No decision, however, was reached. Among the flowers presented for consideration were the mountain laurel, the arbutus, the goldenrod, the dandelion, and the columbine. The latter flower had staunch

FLOWER LORE AND LEGEND

advocates in the members of the Columbine Association, which was organized in Boston about fifteen years ago, and of which Mr. Frederick Le Roy Sargent, instructor in botany at the University of Wisconsin, was chosen president. The movement to memorialize Congress on behalf of the mountain laurel aroused the members of this association to great activity. Numerous reasons were advanced in favor of the columbine. It is a native of nearly every state. The name has the same derivation as Columbus, the discoverer, and as Columbia, which many persons used to think should have been our national name. It displays the national colors. In the South and the Rocky Mountains it is blue, in some parts of the North, white, and in the Middle West, red with a yellow interior. Thus it is emblematic of the blood and wealth which have been poured out in the development of this great country. It has decorative possibilities surpassed by no other flower. Ruskin, in his Elements of Drawing, chose its leaf as a happy illustration of the beauty of a well-ordered subordination of parts.

He demonstrated that each leaf is composed of thirteen lobes, with each lobe perfect and independent, but each yielding something of its own dignity to the formation of the harmonious whole, represents most aptly the motto, e pluribus unum, and is suggestive of the thirteen original states, as they are represented by the stripes upon our national flag. The fancied resemblance of its five long spurs to horns of plenty and of parts of the blossom to the dove, the emblem of peace, and to the eagle, the emblem of fearlessness, tends to make it a floral device that would compare favorably with those of other great nations. Colorado, by act of the legislature, has adopted it as her state flower. In olden times it was regarded as typical of infidelity, and like the willow, it was the emblem of a deserted lover. Sir Thomas Browne, in the seventeenth century, wrote:

"The columbine by lonely wanderer taken,

Is there ascribed to such as are forsaken."

In an old play, written- by Chapman in 1600, it is referred to as a symbol of ingratitude. "What's that, a columbine?"; "No, that thankless flower grows not in my garden."

Shakespeare also uses it as symbolical of ingratitude. Other English poets have referred to it as representing sorrow or desolation, but our American poets have shown a more cheerful appreciation of its charms, and tributes of affection and admiration have come from many of our foremost writers:

"A woodland walk,
A quest of river grapes, a mocking thrush,
A wild rose or a rock-loving columbine
Salve my worst wounds."

Emerson.

FLOWER LORE AND LEGEND

THE GOLDENROD

PRECAUTION - ENCOURAGEMENT

"I lie among the goldenrod,
I love to see it lean and nod;
I love to feel the grassy sod
Whose kindly breast will hold me last,
Whose patient arms will fold me fast!
Fold me from sunshine and from song,
Fold me from sorrow and from wrong,
Through gleaming gates of goldenrod
I'll pass into the rest of God."

Mary Clemmer Ames.

"Because its sun-shaped blossoms show
How souls receive the light of God,
And unto earth give back that glow,
I thank Him for the goldenrod."

Lucy Larcom.

Some years ago, when the subject of a national flower was under consideration, Louis Prang, of Boston, the artist, published a pamphlet setting forth the respective merits of the goldenrod and the arbutus as competitors for the place of honor. He asked for an expression of opinion from the public, and the response was overwhelmingly in favor of the goldenrod. It is without doubt the most representative wild flower in America and is a native of almost every state in the Union. There are one hundred varieties, ninety-five of which are natives of North America. The scientific name of the plant is solidago, from solidus and ago, meaning 'to make solid,' or to draw together,

FLOWER LORE AND LEGEND

which adds to its appropriateness as an emblem of our great republic. In five states, Alabama, Iowa, Missouri, Nebraska, and Pennsylvania, it has been chosen for the state flower. Only two or three varieties grow wild in Europe. One that is quite common in Great Britain is a tall, straight variety called clamis rod. It was formerly known as wound weed on account of its healing properties. A sixteenth century botanist writes that it was dried and in that condition brought from abroad and sold by the herb women in the market in Queen Elizabeth's time. It was in great demand for dressing wounds and cuts, and sold for as much as half a crown an ounce, until the plant was discovered growing wild near certain ponds in Hampstead. Then being native, it became valueless. "This," says the old botanist, "varifieth our English proverb, 'Far fetch and deare bought is best for ladies.'"

Fradslim classes the goldenrod among the plants used by the Druids as divining rods. In skilled hands the plant is credited with being able to point out springs of fresh water, as well as hidden treasures of gold and silver. In New Zealand and St. Helena the flower is known as yellow weed and one variety grows to be more than eight feet high, with branches like a tree. In medicine it is used to relieve nausea and spasmodic pains. The cattle avoid it on account of it's astringency. Beverage made from it was called blue mountain tea. At one time it produced oils and dyes. While, like most Americans, it can name an ancestry that had its origin in an older country, it is distinctly American. It holds no place in the mythology of the ancients and its associations are almost all with the new world. As the daisy and buttercup are so closely associated that one hardly can think of one without the other, so the goldenrod and the aster are almost inseparable, not only in fact, but also in legend and tradition. In a queer little hut, on the edge of a pine forest and beside a clear lake, lived an old Indian squaw. She had lived there so long that no one knew when she came, and all sorts of queer tales were told about her by the few people who

FLOWER LORE AND LEGEND

approached her abode. It was said that she had the power of changing human beings into animals, birds, or plants, and that she could talk to all things that lived in the forest in their own language. She was so old that she was bent almost double. Her face was wrinkled, but her eyes were bright and seemed to see things. She sat all day in the door of her hut weaving mats and baskets, but no one ever knew what she did with them. One day late in the summer two children were seen wandering along the shore of the lake. They skipped from stone to stone, and gathered the flowers that grew almost to the water's edge. At last they sat down to rest.

One of them had beautiful golden hair, and her companion, who had soft, deep-blue eyes that looked like stars, called her Golden-hair. They had heard of the squaw and her magical powers, and as they sat by the lake they talked of what they would choose to be, if she should try her spells upon them. Golden-hair wished to be something that would make every one who saw it happy and cheerful, while timid little Star-eye wished that she might be near her friend. At last the sun began to sink in the west. The wind stirred among the tree-tops and every now and then the acorns fell with a noise like raindrops, and the little girls began to get frightened. They saw the hut in the distance and holding each other's hands they ran toward it. As they drew near the old woman worked faster than ever and pretended that she did not see them. The children came quite close to her and Golden-hair said: "Please, can you tell me where the old woman lives who can make us whatever we wish to be?" The Indian, looking up, said: "Perhaps I can. What do you want of her?"; "I want," said the child, "to ask her to make me into something that will please everybody, and Star-eye wants to be always near to me."; "Come in," said the squaw "and sit down. I will give you each a cake made of Indian corn, and when you have eaten it we will talk about your wishes."" The little girls were half afraid, but did not like to decline, so they went into the hut and sat down

FLOWER LORE AND LEGEND

to eat their cake. That was a long time ago, and no one has ever seen those children since, but the next morning there were two new field flowers blossoming in the fields, on the prairies, and on the mountain sides; one was like a bright yellow plume that waved in the wind and glowed like gold in the sunshine, and the other was a little starry, purple flower. The two are never very far apart and they are called goldenrod and aster. Mindful, perhaps, of this, Bryant wrote: But on the hill the goldenrod, and the aster in the wood, And the yellow sunflower by the brook, in autumn beauty stood. Both in legendary lore and in literature tributes to the goldenrod are confined almost entirely to American writers, but it lacks not for eulogy. Every time the national flower discussion is renewed much is written, both of prose and poetry, in appreciation of its beauty, and the great among us have not deemed it unworthy of their best efforts. Longfellow, Whittier, Lowell, and Bayard Taylor have all helped to swell the chorus of love and praise of the flower. Celia Thaxter, Elaine Goodale, Lucy Larcom, and Helen Hunt Jackson have added their words of affection. One who has laid down his pen, and of whom it has been said that he was our 'unofficial poet laureate,' has told that it is at its best in August and September.

> "Grows a weed
> More richly here beside our mellow seas
> That is the autumn's harbinger and pride,
> When fades the cardinal flower, whose red heart bloom
> Glows like a living coal upon the green
> Of the midsummer meadows, then how bright,
> How deepening bright like mounting flame doth burn,
> The goldenrod upon a thousand hills!
> This is the autumn's flower, and to my soul
> A token fresh of beauty and of life,
> And life's supreme delight."

Richard Watson Gilder, An Autumn Meditation.

FLOWER LORE AND LEGEND

THE GENTIAN

CLOSED, SWEET DREAMS - FRINGED, I LOOK TO HEAVEN

"Beside the brook, on the umbered meadow,
Where yellow fern-tufts fleck the faded ground,
With folded lids beneath the palmy shadow
The gentian nods in dewy slumbers bound.

Upon those soft-fringed lids the bee sits brooding,
Like a fond lover, loth to say farewell,
Or with shut wings through silken folds intruding,
Creeps near the heart his drowsy tale to tell."

Sarah H. Whitman.

There was a King of Ulyria named Gentius who reigned at the same time that Perseus was King of Macedonia. Being of a cruel and tyrannical nature, and much given to self-indulgence, he made no attempt to control the piratical attacks which his subjects made from time to time upon the Romans, and when ambassadors were sent from Rome to remonstrate with him he put them in prison. Upon war being declared between Rome and Macedonia, he offered his services to Perseus for a sum of money. The latter agreed to his terms, but afterward, when the war was actually begun, refused to keep the contract. Gentius assembled his forces, but the war was terminated in less than thirty days by the victorious Romans, and the King and his family were taken prisoners and carried to Rome to grace the triumph of Amicius, the general. Gentius was a student of botany and he is reported to have been the first to discover the medicinal qualities of the plant which bears his name and which grew most luxuriantly in his kingdom.

FLOWER LORE AND LEGEND

At that time there were thirteen remedies that were credited to it. It was said to be an antidote for poison, for the bites of mad dogs and of venomous reptiles, and was regarded as most efficacious for diseases of the liver. A wine in which the leaves had been steeped was considered very refreshing for persons over-wearied or chilled by exposure. Although this was centuries ago, today it still holds an important place in pharmacy. The root is very bitter and is used for the purposes of a tonic. A story is told of the curative powers of the plant, which dates from the eleventh century. During the reign of Ladislas, surnamed the saint, the whole of Hungary was devastated by a terrible plague. Having heard the story of Charlemagne and the thistle, the good King prayed that when he discharged an arrow into the air it might be guided to some plant that could be successfully used to check the devastating disease. He shot the arrow and it was found piercing a gentian root. The remedy was at once tried and the results were astonishingly successful. The fringed gentian is one of the most beautiful wild flowers that grows. There is a yellow variety, but generally the color is of a most dazzling blue. Thoreau says: "It surpasses the back of the male bluebird." Artists have regarded it as the nearest approach to the color of the sky. Spirit blue is made from coal tar, but it is often improperly called gentian blue.

There are one hundred and eighty different species, the most beautiful, according to recent authorities, being native in the United States. It blooms in the autumn and is about the last of the wild flowers: Thoreau records having found one as late as November, although they are in their prime from the middle to the last of September. The fringed gentian has been a rival of the arbutus and the goldenrod for the honor of being our national flower and it has had many supporters. Hosmer speaks of its modesty:

"The varied aster tribes enclose

FLOWER LORE AND LEGEND

Bright eyes in autumn's smoky bower,
And azure cup the gentian shows,
A modest little flower."

It is the state flower of Wyoming. It grows in profusion among the Alps of Switzerland and the following story was told by the much-loved Dean Stanley. When traveling in Switzerland in 18 18 he arrived at the village of Martigny a few days after the terrible catastrophe which was occasioned that year by the overflowing of the Danube. His curiosity being excited, he determined to climb the mountain and learn by personal observation the extent of the calamity. It was represented to him that the road was passable for horses, but upon reaching a certain ford it was found that the water had risen so that passage was impossible. "Is there no other way?" he inquired of the guides. He was told that there was one other way, but that it took steady nerves and a strong head, "for if you slip you are lost," they said. He signified his willingness to try it, and it was not until it was too late to retreat that he realized the danger of the undertaking. He wrote that, while creeping slowly along a narrow ledge of rock, where the least misstep would have sent him headlong into the valley below, just as he was struggling with an almost irresistible impulse to look down, which would have been his undoing, he espied, growing out of the rocks above him, a cluster of beautiful blue gentians. While looking up at them he seemed to forget his danger; his nerves steadied themselves, and he passed over the perilous crossing safely. Always after that it was a flower dear to his heart.

Besides the fringed gentian there is a variety known as the closed, or bottle, gentian. The blossoms are shaped like the thick part of a tiny Indian club and a number, generally five or six, are gathered together at the narrow neck of the club and rise from the green cushion like a beautiful rosette. These blossoms never open, and it is said that at one time all gentians were closed, but the fringed gentian is accounted for in this way: Once upon a time the Queen of the Fairies was out very late. It was Allhallows eve, which is the last day in October, and she had been so busy that she had not realized how fast the time had flown. It was after midnight and the moon, upon which the fairies depend for light, had sunk down out of sight. The fireflies had gone to bed. The little Queen was frightened almost to death and, hurrying up to a gentian, she asked if she might sleep in its blossom until morning. The flower was sleepy and did not like being wakened, so it asked rather crossly, "Who are you?"; "I am the Queen of the Fairies," was the answer. "Well, if you are the Queen, you ought to be able to find places enough to sleep," said the selfish blossom, and went to sleep again. The fairy looked all around and saw nothing but gentians. It was very late in the season and all the other flowers had gone. She thought she would try one more, and going up to another, she timidly asked for shelter for the night. "Poor little thing," it said, "come in and let me cover you up till the sun comes out." The tired Queen crept in and slept soundly until morning. As soon as the sun was up she hastened away, but before she left she said to the kind flower, "You are my dear friend and from this time you and all your children shall be different from the other gentians. I will bestow upon you the power to open and enjoy the beams of the sun and the refreshing dew." Then she kissed the flower- fairies do not know anything about germs- and ever since then the fringed gentian opens with the morning light and closes as night comes on.

The gentian has not attracted much attention from the English poets. Wordsworth and Montgomery both allude to its wonderful coloring. However, it is firmly rooted in American literature and many tributes have been paid to the unique beauty of both varieties.

"Thou blossom bright with autumn dew,

FLOWER LORE AND LEGEND

And colored with the heaven's own blue,
That openest when the quiet light
Succeeds the keen and frosty night.

Then doth thy sweet and quiet eye
Look through its fringes to the sky,
Blue- blue- as if that sky let fall
A flower from its cerulean wall.

I would that thus, when I shall see
The hour of death draw near to me,
Hope, blossoming within my heart,
May look to heaven as I depart."

Bryant. Ode to a Fringed Gentian.

FLOWER LORE AND LEGEND

THE CHRYSANTHEMUM

WEALTH - ABUNDANCE

"Fair gift of friendship! and her ever bright
And faultless image! welcome now thou art,
In thy pure loveliness- thy robes of white,
Speaking a moral to the feeling heart;
Unscathed by heats- by wintry blasts unmoved-
Thy strength thus tested- and thy charms improved."

Anna Peyre Dinnies, To a White Chrysanthemum.

"In the second month the peach tree blooms,
But not till the ninth the chrysanthemums;
So each must wait till his own time comes."

Translation from Japanese.

Of all flowers the chrysanthemum may justly be called the queen of autumn, and it is difficult to believe that this royal blossom is own cousin to the modest little daisy that blooms so unobtrusively by the roadside. As it is known to-day, it is the product, not of nature, but of art, and it has been brought to its present state of perfection mainly by the efforts of the florists of China and Japan. It is a native of China. Originally it was yellow and the other colors which make it so showy and popular have come from cultivation. The name is derived from two Greek words, which mean golden flower. Its month is October. An old Chinese chronicle of the eleventh century tells of a plant which produced both large and small blossoms. Some had yellow centers, from which radiated white petals, while others were wholly yellow. Confucius mentions it in his Li-ki, but any information that can be gathered is fragmentary and incomplete.

FLOWER LORE AND LEGEND

It is the national floral emblem of Japan, although some writers contend that the place of honor should belong to the cherry blossom. The following legend of the origin of the flower is found in Japanese folk-lore:

One beautiful moonlight night a young girl, wandering in a garden, gathered a blossom and began to pull off the petals one by one to see whether her lover cared for her or not. Suddenly a little elf stood before her, and after assuring her that she was passionately adored, he added: "Your love will become your husband, and will live as many years as the flower, which you may choose, has petals." He then disappeared, and the maiden began her search for a flower which should have the greatest number of petals. At length she picked a Persian carnation, and with a gold hairpin she separated each petal into two or three parts. Soon her deft fingers had increased the number of folioles of the corolla to three times the original number, and she wept with joy to think of the happiness she had been the means of assuring her future husband. And so the Ki-Ku, as the Japanese call it, was created hundreds of years ago in a garden, with the moon shining over the flowers, the streams, and the little bamboo bridges. The Kiku-no-sekku, or festival of the chrysanthemum, is held during the ninth month, which, according to the old calendar, is about the last of October, and as the birthday of the Emperor fell upon the third of November, that day has become a gala day in all parts of the empire and the occasion of wonderful floral displays. At Dango Zaka, one of the suburbs of Tokio, is held a most unique exhibition. Under canopies of matting and sometimes on revolving stages, are arranged life-size figures made entirely of chrysanthemums, with the exception of the face and hands, which are formed of some sort of composition. The figures are grouped as tableaux representing historical or legendary scenes. They are most curiously made of split bamboo, in which the roots and stems of the plants are packed in damp earth and bound around with straw, while the flowers are drawn through the frame and woven into the desired pattern. By careful sprinkling every evening the flowers are kept fresh for the month during which the festival continues.

In some instances small figures are used to depict events of current interest. At the time of the Japanese-Russian war battlefields were shown where cavalry, infantry, bridges, and scenery were all composed of flowers. The fact that there are about eight hundred varieties of the flower, with almost three hundred different shades of color, varying in size from gigantic to microscopic, makes this wonderful display of living pictures a credit to Japanese ingenuity. Two imperial garden parties are given by the Emperor each year; one when the cherry blossoms are in bloom and the other at the height of the chrysanthemum season. A few days before the entertainment each guest receives a large card ornamented with a yellow blossom, inviting him, by the order of the Emperor and Empress, to attend the chrysanthemum party, which is to be held at a stated time in the imperial gardens. The entertainment consists of viewing the display of flowers. Members of the court circle compose poems for the occasion upon subjects assigned by the Emperor. A collation is served on the lawn and a liquor is passed, in which chrysanthemums have been dipped, and the Mikado's health is drunk to the following toast:

"Let the Emperor live forever! May he see the chrysanthemum cup go around autumn after autumn for a thousand years!"

A golden chrysanthemum of sixteen petals, somewhat conventionalized, has long been the official crest of the Emperor, and since the revolution of 1868, when the Mikado was restored to his original power, it has come into its own again. It is embroidered on flags and banners and appears on all government documents. The soldiers of the imperial army wear it as a frontal on their caps.

Among other innovations which modern Japan has adopted from Europe are orders of knighthood or decorations for military and other services. Of these the Order of the Chrysanthemum is the highest. It was instituted by the late Mikado in 1876 and is bestowed only on sovereigns and those of royal birth. Only three subjects below imperial rank have been invested with it, Marshals Yamagata and Oyama, and Prince Ito. The emblem consists of a star in the form of a cross, with thirty two rays. In each of the angles formed by the four principal arms is a chrysanthemum. The ribband is red, with violet edges, and the emblem is attached by a gold chrysanthemum. In Japanese art and ornamentation the chrysanthemum is a most frequent theme, and it is profusely made use of in all forms. In one of the apartments in the royal palace the decorations consist solely of paintings and carvings of the Ki-ku. The fox and the Ki-ku are often associated and a legend is given as the explanation. A fox assuming the form of a beautiful woman attracted the attention of a certain Prince, who fell deeply in love with her and sought to make her his wife.

One day she fell asleep in a bed of chrysanthemums, which counteracted the enchantment, and for the time. she resumed her natural shape. The Prince, seeing the fox, shot, hitting the animal in the forehead. Afterward, seeing that his sweetheart had a wound corresponding to the one he had given the fox, he discovered her true nature and immediately renounced her. Another favorite motif of decoration is the chrysanthemum blossom floating in running water, and this is also explained by a legend. There lived many hundred years ago a youth named Jido, who was a great favorite with the Chinese Emperor, Muh-Wang, who appointed him chief of his attendants and taught him a sentence from Buddha insuring him long life and safety. One day Jido was passing the imperial couch and accidentally touched one of the pillows with his foot. A jealous rival reported the fact to the ruler, who banished the youth. In the province of Kia, in Japan, is a hill which is called Chrysanthemum Mount, because the flower grows there so luxuriantly. It overhangs a clear river. Thither went Jido and spent his time from morning until night painting on the petals of the blossoms the sentence which the Chinese Emperor had taught him. These petals dropped into the river and changed the water into the elixir of life. There is only one place in Japan where the Ki-ku is not cultivated, and that is in Himeji, and Lafcadio Hearn gives as the reason this legend: In Himeji is a great castle with thirty turrets, whose owner possessed great wealth. One of the chief maid-servants was named O-Kiku, which means chrysanthemum blossom. Many costly things were in her care and among them ten gold dishes of great value. One day one of these could not be found and the maid, knowing that she was responsible and not being able to prove her innocence, drowned herself. After that every night her ghost could be heard slowly counting the dishes, Ich-mai, Ni-mai, Sen-mai. When she came to ten there would be a despairing cry, which was followed by the counting. Her spirit, it is said, passed into the body of a curious little insect, whose head resembles a woman's with disheveled hair. The Japanese name of the insect means the fly of O-Kiku, and it is to be found nowhere but in Himeji. This legend has been dramatized and is still presented in all the popular theaters under the title of "The Manor of the Dish of O-Kiku." It is most unlucky to even carry a chrysanthemum into Himeji.

The gold flower of the Greeks was no doubt a small variety of the chrysanthemum, and, on account of its lasting quality, was used by the ancients to make chaplets for their gods. Eleven remedies were derived from the plant, most of which were for local applications. They also used to scatter the leaves among clothing to protect it from insects. It is interesting to note

FLOWER LORE AND LEGEND

that since 1903 the use of chrysanthemum powder for the destruction of mosquitoes has been recommended by our Department of Agriculture. An article on the subject by A. L. Heuera, of Mexico, was published by the Bureau of Ethnology in 1907. Eben Rexford, in beautiful verse, refers to the chrysanthemum as the last autumn flower:

> "Lo! in the corner yonder
> There's a gleam of white and gold-
> The gold of summer's sunshine,
> The white of winter's cold.
> And laden with spicy odors,
> The autumn breezes come
> From the nooks and corners, brightened
> By the brave chrysanthemum."

The first chrysanthemum introduced into Europe was sent from China to Blanchard, a Marseilles merchant. It created such a sensation that the attention of the East India Company was attracted, and it at once began importing other varieties. In 1842, Robert Fortune was sent to China and Japan by the Royal Horticultural Society, and on his return brought with him two small varieties of the Chusan daisy, from which have sprung the wonderful pom poms that are now so much admired. The first public exhibition was held in England in 1846 and from that time began the era of the chrysanthemum outside the Orient. One of the greatest attractions of London in November each year is the display at the Temple and Inner Temple Gardens. These exhibitions have been held annually since 1850. There is no authentic record as to the first introduction of the flower to America, but the late Peter Henderson, a noted horticulturist, was the first to import directly from Japan about 1860. Since that time the displays in this country have equaled any outside of China and Japan. There has been organized since 1890 the Chrysanthemum Society of America, which by its last report

FLOWER LORE AND LEGEND

supplied a list of nearly three thousand varieties, with the names of the producers or importers. In one nursery in California six hundred varieties of the flower are cultivated. No flower except the rose has been written about so extensively as the chrysanthemum. Over one hundred books have been published concerning it, most of which are quite expensive as works of art and decoration. It has not, however, figured frequently in poetry; even in a collection of one hundred poems translated from the Japanese there is only one reference to the national flower. Its lack of perfume has been remarked upon.

> "It cheers with bloom the stormy gloom
> By chill December nursed;
> And it is told in stories old
> That this fair blossom first,
> On that fair morn when Christ was born,
> Into white beauty burst.
>
> Perhaps- ah, well, we cannot tell
> If truly it be so;
> I but repeat the legend sweet,
> And only this I know-
> That in the prime of Christmas time
> The Christ's sweet flowers blow."

Elizabeth Akers, Chrysanthemum.

FLOWER LORE AND LEGEND

THE ROSEMARY

REMEMBRANCE

"The boar's head in hand I bear,
Bedecked with bays and rosemary,
And I pray you my masters, 'be merry.'"

Old Carol.

"There's rosemary for you, that's for remembrance;
Pray you, love, remember."

Shakespeare, Hamlet.

The rosemary may be called a versatile flower. It has been associated with life and death, with joy and sorrow. It has decorated with its luxuriant foliage the garden walls of proud Hampton Court, and has thrived in many a kitchen garden. It belongs to the mint family and was accorded a most honorable place among the ancients. The Latin calls it rosamarius, meaning dew of the sea, because it grows so luxuriantly near the seashore and also because the foliage has a silvery appearance as if covered with dew. It is said that the gray bushes along the rocky coasts of France and Italy well warrant the name. It was also called Mary's rose and was an emblem of the Virgin. The Greeks and Romans made garlands of it with which they crowned the guests of honor at their feasts. They also burned it as incense at many of their religious ceremonies. During the Palilia, or Shepherd's Festival, which was held in April to celebrate the founding of Rome by the shepherds and husbandmen, rosemary and laurel in large quantities were burned that the smoke might purify the sacred groves and fountains from unintentional pollution by the flocks and herds. It was one of the herbs used by the Romans in embalming their dead and its evergreen leaves symbolized to them the immortality of the soul. When they invaded Briton they brought with them many of their old rites and superstitions, and this may account for its popularity as a funeral emblem. Until comparatively recently in many parts of rural England it was strewn upon the coffin and sprays of rosemary were distributed to all those who attended the service that they might be cast into the grave as a final ceremony, emblematic of the life to come. One of the most pathetic incidents connected with the funeral of Princess Alice of Hesse was when a poor old peasant woman of the Odenwald timidly laid her little wreath of rosemary beside the rare and costly flowers that covered the casket. In spite of its association with the dead, as an emblem of memory and faithfulness the rosemary was in great demand as a bridal flower. Herrick refers to its double use when he said:

> "Grow for two ends, it matters not at all,
> Be't for my bridal or my burial."

It was customary for the bride to wear several sprays twined in her bridal wreath by some member of her family, to silently remind her to take with her to her new home memories of the dear old roof-tree and the loving hearts she was leaving behind. It was a token of gladness as well as of the dignity of the marriage sacrament. The bridal bed was decked with its sprays. The young men and maidens who attended the happy couple all wore or carried sprigs of rosemary, but it was to be borne in the heart as well as in the hand. Mystically it was thought to strengthen both the memory and the heart and to signify love and loyalty. In an old play is found the question: "Was the rosemary dipped?" This refers to the custom of dipping a spray in the wine cup before drinking to the bridal couple.

In Miss Strickland's description of the wedding of the

unfortunate Anne of Cleves to Henry VIII, it is said that the Queen wore a coronet of gold and gems in which was fastened a spray of rosemary, "that herb of grace which was worn by maidens both at weddings and funerals."

At his first appearance on his wedding day the bridegroom was presented by the bridesmaids with a bunch of rosemary tied with white satin ribband, indicating the authority of the bride in the household. Wherever the plant grew in the garden, in that house it was a common saying that the "Mistress was master," or as another proverb expresses it, "Where rosemary flourishes in the garden, the gray mare is the better horse." This superstition may account for the fact that the plant is not now so prominent a feature in gardens as it used to be. The following charm was said to be very potent:

On the eve of St. Magdalene three maidens all under twenty-one must be gathered in the bed chamber of one of the number and together must prepare a mixture of wine, vinegar, and water in a ground glass vessel. Each maid must take three sips of the liquid, into which she must dip a spray of rosemary to be placed in her bosom. They must then all go silently to sleep in the same bed. One spoken word will break the charm. If the conditions were carefully complied with the dream of each, it was said, would reveal her fate. Among the early Britons the herb was held to be of great importance in the observance of Christmas. The wassail bowl, which was passed around the banqueting hall, was wreathed, the night before, with rosemary, and the boar's head, the first dish to be served on Christmas day, and which was carried with great state to the central table, was trimmed with the same plant. The association with Christmas may have been suggested by an old Spanish tradition that when the Mother was escaping with the Child Jesus from Herod's soldiers, some of the plants among which they passed rustled and crackled, thus betraying the travelers; but a tall rosemary bush

FLOWER LORE AND LEGEND

stretched out its branches like arms and the Mother and Child found refuge in its thick foliage. There is also a legend that the linen and little frocks of the Holy Child were spread upon a rosemary bush to dry. When the Virgin came to get them she found she had hung them upon a sunbeam. Thus it became Mary's rose and was thought to bring peace and good will to every family who numbered it among their Christmas adornments.

The plant was cultivated extensively throughout England in the monastic gardens on account of its curative properties. It was said to be beneficial for all disorders of the liver and for convulsions from any cause. A liniment was made from it that was used for gout. Mixed with honey it was in demand for bronchial troubles. Cervantes tells a story that a young man was once bitten by dogs at a gypsy camp. The Queen took hairs from the dogs, fried them in oil, and laid the product on the wound. Next she laid on green rosemary, which she had chewed to a pulp, and then binding up the leg with cloth, she made the sign of the cross over the bite, and a quick cure was the result. Timbs says that rosemary water was called "the bath of life."

In some verses, which are known as The Bride's Good Morrow, its use at marriage is pictured:

> "Young men and maids do ready stand
> With sweet rosemary in their hand,
> A perfect token of your virgin's life,
> To wait upon you they attend,
> Unto the church to make an end,
> And God make thee a joyful wife."

In contrast, Gray sets out in rhyme the funeral custom:

> "To show their love the neighbors far and near,

FLOWER LORE AND LEGEND

Followed with wistful look the damsel's bier.
Sprigged rosemary the lads and lassies bore,
While dismally the parson walked before."

Briesly, in his Chronicles, thus vividly described the scene at the burial of a huntsman, whose fellows attended with the dogs: The old huntsmen gathered round the grave in a solid ring, each holding his dog by the slip, and when the final ashes to ashes, dust to dust was pronounced, the whole strewed their sprigs of rosemary over the coffin, then raising their heads, gave a simultaneous "Yahoo! tally-ho!" the sound of which became heightened by the dogs joining their voices as they rung the last cry over their earthed companion.

In old days the rosemary was sometimes called guard robe, because it was strewn in chests of clothing to keep out the moths. After the great division in the church the names of many plants were changed in the hope of obliterating the scientific and medical knowledge of the monks. But the name of this flower was too sacred to be taken away. The Italians recommended it for the preservation of youth and to strengthen the memory, and there was an old belief that if it was used in the bath it would impart gaiety and sprightliness. Young women considered it very effective in the removal of freckles. In Hungary a medicinal water is distilled from the plant which is esteemed as a remedy for nervous troubles. A fine aromatic oil is obtained from it in America and England which is of value in manufacturing perfumes. The plant is also cultivated for the use of the bees, the honey extracted from it being of an excellent quality.

The fairies, too, claim an interest in the rosemary. In Scandinavia it is called ellegrim, which means elfin plant. It is said that the little elves hide in its branches when they are having their frolics, or when they are caught in a storm. There is no plant that the Italian and Spanish fairies care more for. In fact, with all fairies it is really quite a national flower, and the reason is that it hides and protects them under all circumstances. Once upon a time there was a Queen who was very unhappy because she had no children. As she was walking in her garden she saw a beautiful rosemary bush and she wept bitterly, saying, "Even this plant has branches and blossoms, while I who long for a child have none." The next morning when she awoke she was surprised to see the plant by her bedside. She had it potted and cared for it herself, spraying it with milk several times a day. Her nephew, who was King of Spain, came to visit her, and noticing what care she took of it imagined that it must be something very rare, so he stole it and took it with him when he returned to his kingdom. One day when he was playing on the flute he was astonished to see a beautiful Princess emerge from the bush. He was so startled that he dropped his flute, and the maiden disappeared. The King was very unhappy for he had immediately fallen desperately in love with his beautiful visitor. Being called by state affairs, he entrusted his precious plant to the special custody of his head gardener, with instructions to guard it most securely. His sisters were in the garden one day and amused themselves by playing on his flute. Again the beautiful young girl stepped out of the rosemary bush.

The sisters, who were jealous of her beauty and regarded her as an intruder, struck her. From that time the plant began to droop and wither. The gardener, fearing the anger of the King, fled into the wood, and at midnight he overheard two dragons talking to each other. In the course of the conversation one dragon remarked that the rosemary could only be restored by sprinkling it with dragon's blood. When the man heard this he immediately attacked and killed them, and taking some of the blood poured it on the roots of the plant, thereby breaking the spell and bringing to life the Princess Rosa Maria, who had been invisibly chained by an enchantment, which could only be interrupted by the music from a flute. The King soon came back

FLOWER LORE AND LEGEND

and they were married with great splendor and lived happily ever after. The rosemary has had a place in literature in both ancient and modern times. The early English writers especially make numerous references to it. Chaucer and Spenser both allude to its popularity.

Shakespeare makes use of it in several of his plays, which show a familiarity with its traditions. Drayton, in his quaint language, has much to say about the flower. Herrick and Gay have both given it an honored place among their floral symbols. Shenstone expresses indignation at the disrespect shown to the rosemary in modern times, while Tom Moore sings of it in mournful strains.

> "Come funeral flower! sweet-scented flower,
> Come press my lips, and lie with me
> Beneath the lovely alder tree,
> And we will sleep a pleasant sleep,
> And not a care shall dare intrude,
> To break the marble solitude,
> So peaceful and so deep."

Henry Kirke White, To the Herb Rosemary.

FLOWER LORE AND LEGEND

L'ENVOI

"Et si la vie est un passage,
Sur ce passage
Au moins semones des fleurs."

Moncreiff, Couplets Detaches.

"And if life be but a passage,
On the passage
Let us strew some flowers."

Translation.

Henry Ward Beecher once told a story of a little bud who thought she could not unfold when springtime came:

And the sun and the wind laughed, for they knew that when they should shine and blow upon the bud and fill up and swell those tiny leaves, it would open from the necessity of its nature. An anonymous writer wisely wrote:

"Children are simple, loving, true,
'Tis Heaven that made them so,
And would you teach them, be so too,
And stoop to what they know.
Begin with simple lessons, things,
On which they love to look,
Flowers, pebbles, insects, birds on wings.
These are God's spelling-book.
And children know His a, b, c,
As bees, where flowers set.
Wouldst thou a skilful teacher be
Learn then this alphabet."

FLOWER LORE AND LEGEND

About 1324 there was established by the troubadours, at Toulouse, in France, a flower festival at which prizes were awarded by judges selected to pass upon the merits of all original poems, which might be submitted to the competition. Each contributor was required to prove originality. The prize awarded was a golden violet. Although women were barred from the contest, because it was believed that no woman could produce anything original, Lady Clemence Isaure, of high lineage, gave the bulk of her fortune to permanently endow an institution, which, under the name of the College of the Gay Science, took charge of the contests and the annual floral celebrations. When her father strenuously objected to the attentions of her knight, in bidding him farewell, from the castle battlements, she threw him a violet, that the exile might wear her color, an eglantine (the sweetbrier), her favorite flower, as a love token, and a marigold, as an earnest of her faith in him. The castle being attacked the knight came to the rescue, but was killed, with her father, just after their reconciliation. She never married.

The festival was celebrated for 450 years, and, after a time, silver eglantines and marigolds were also awarded, as second and third prizes. Some writers have referred to this festival as a continuation of the Floralia, by which the goddess Flora was honored at Rome, in rites adopted not only from the Greek, but also from more ancient nations. Flower revels, like those of the Romans, were celebrated among Asiatics, Goths, Celts, Saxons, and Scandinavians.

The Mayday festivities of England, Scotland, Wales, Ireland, the Normans, and modern continental nations, are believed to be a survival of the old Floralia. It is certain that all races of men have taken part in honoring and rejoicing over the flowers, and the return of the flowering season. The stories that are gathered here, though not original, have been given a new dress with the hope to freshen interest in legendary lore, now almost obsolete, because inaccessible.

> "Methought that of these visionary flowers,
> I made a nosegay, bound in such a way,
> That the same hues, which in their natural bowers,
> Were mingled or opposed, the like array,
> Kept these imprisoned children of the hours
> Within my hand- and then elate and gay,
> I hastened to the spot, whence I had come,
> That I might there present it; oh! to whom?"

Shelley, Wild Flowers.

THE END

Printed in Great Britain
by Amazon